A HISTORY of CANVEY ISLAND

Fred McCave

IAN HENRY PUBLICATIONS

ISBN 0 86025 894 7

Cover illustration:
Post Office and pump. The Red Cow is on the extreme left of the picture.

Printed and Bound in Great Britain by
J W Arrowsmith Ltd., Bristol
for
Ian Henry Publications Ltd.,
38 Parkstone Avenue, Hornchurch, Essex RM11 3LW

Poised off Shellhaven Point in the Thames Estuary is Canvey Island, an area unique in Britain. Its chronicles stretch back to pre-Roman times, while its present development contains some of the latest technological marvels of the age.

Romans used it, Danes fought round it, the Dutch embanked and also invaded it. More than once the cruel sea has smashed its way in and has been triumphantly ejected, not without fearful loss of life and damage. Twice in a life-time it has been a focal point in the country's defence. Deep water anchorages and potential wharfage have attracted the attentions of the oil moguls and this has sparked off fierce resistance from some of the Island's inhabitants.

Before disinterring its past, let us consider its present situation. Under nationwide local government reorganisation the Canvey Urban District ceased on 1 April, 1974, and twinned with adjacent Benfleet to become Castle Point District Council, a title devised by a local resident from Hadleigh CASTLE and The POINT (an area of marshland at the eastern end of Canvey Island). In 1985 Canvey's population was 36,500 and it had 4,421 acres inside its 14 miles of bastion seawall. A total of 44 miles are maintained by the Council. Now well below sea level, it was at one time higher, had a different shape and extended further into the Thames than it now does.

In pre-historic times the Island was part of a coastal forest area, without cultivation, but this changed with the Roman invasion of 43 A.D. An early map-maker, Claudius Ptolemaeus Ptolemy, geographer of Alexandria (90 - 168 A.D.), showed the area as a series of islands and named it Cnossos (Robert Morden [circa 1700] rendered this as Conventus).

There is ample evidence of Roman use, which can be divided into three - military, maritime and industrial. Dealing with the first, on Upper Horse Island in Hole Haven Creek are earthworks of Roman origin, which were part of a fortified camp. Traces of a Roman port, with the strong possibility of a lighthouse, at the eastern tip of the Island account for the seafaring side. The industrial use is the most extensive: they are known as 'red hills' and there are about 200 of them in Essex. They have been researched over a long period and various reasons have been advanced for their use. The verdict is that they were used for, among other things, producing salt by evaporation and in almost all cases (except for one to which I shall refer later) they are on the fringes of the tide. The mineral was a valuable commodity and would have had a great deal of importance for the Romans. Recently an inland salt-making works has been discovered on the Island, pointing to the fact that in those days Canvey was of a different shape and what has now been safely gathered behind its walls was then part of the littoral. Some idea of its importance can be gained from the fact that this latest find is included in a site of 4.2 acres and is a scheduled ancient monument. It is one of six such sites preserved in the country.

Workings such as these could well justify the establishment of a port, its armed protection and a highway. Although there is no direct evidence of paved ways, a road could have existed to Wickford*.

An exhaustive study of the mysterious Red Hills on Canvey was made by Ernest Linder, B.Sc., who lived on the Island. It was read on 26 November, 1938, published in March, 1939, by the *Essex Naturalist* and republished in booklet form by Castle Point District Council in 1975.

Mr Linder investigated five of the Red Hills and

*On Roman Roads in Essex by Miller Christy. Transactions of the Essex Archaeological Society, 1920. **The Roman and Saxon Settlements, Southend-on-Sea** by William Pollitt, a report compiled for the Public Library & Museum Committee of the Corporation of Southend-on-Sea. Transactions of the Southend-on-Sea & District Antiquarian and Historical Society, 1923.

his conclusions are "All one can say at present is that the geographical position of the sites and the character of the mounds is consistent with their having been occupied during the Romano-British period for the following purposes -

1. The manufacture of crude red pottery.
2. The use of such pottery on the site for the manufacture of salt by evaporation of seawater, and
3. The curing and salting of fish caught in the Estuary." [This latter was a suggestion by M R Hull, Curator of the Colchester Museum]

Mr Linder further says that occupation may have been repeated in mediaeval times.

His pottery collection and other Red Hill finds are vested in the Council. It was donated to the former Canvey Island Urban Council and is now in the custody of Chelmsford and Essex Museum on indefinite loan. As a condition of the loan some items from the collection are kept on display at Canvey Island Dutch Cottage Museum.

When the legions fell back to defend the Imperial City, Canvey was ignored by the Saxons, but not by the Vikings and sea battles took place offshore. When, in 1855, the railway line was extended to Benfleet, remains of Viking long-boats were found in the Creek dividing the mainland from the Island. They had been destroyed by Edward, son of Alfred the Great, in 894. A Danish name is still used at Canvey for Leigh Beck, 'beck' being a Danelaw county term for stream.

I feel that it is very appropriate that the earliest mention about Canvey should come from the High Court Records. For the first, but certainly not the last, time the transfer of land at 'Caneveye' took place in 1254. The spelling was again phonetic when references are made to Kaneveye (1259-60) and Kaneweye (1245-65), in *Fleet of Fines for Essex*.

As the centuries passed, more and more detail became recorded.

At one time the valuable pasture lands were shared by nine mainland parishes - North and South Benfleet, Bowers Gifford, Hadleigh, Laindon, Pitsea, Prittlewell, Southchurch and Vange.

Marshes in the North Benfleet area paid two

Leigh Beck Farm, c.1905

shillings each on 27 June, 1591 towards the repair of
the nave and belfry of North Benfleet Church. In
October, 1597, eight shillings went towards repairing
the church steeple with shingle.

Nicholas Wentworth in 1543 owned Knightswick,
Southwick and Attnash. Edward Baker and James Baker
held 500 acres in 1569 with Sir Roger Appleton. At
those times Canvey can best be judged from one of
Norden's maps of 1594 showing Canuey Ilandes in
three parts. A deep creek was depicted from what is
now Thorney Bay towards Oyster Fleet where, centuries before, the Romans had laid down a bed. One
variety of oyster was named after the Island – Ostres
Canveyensis.

Canvey – cailed Canwaie Iles by William
Harrison, rector of Radwinter, in 1577, when he published his *Description of England* – provided spring
pasture for flocks of fat- tailed sheep. One of them
decorates the Island's own Coat of Arms (Armorial
bearings were granted to the Council on 5 January,
1971, being formally received on 3 April of that year
at a Civic Dinner). The pasturing of these animals
played a significant part in the district's economy and
its fringe industry, ewes' milk, made into cheese. The
industry was abandoned in 1720 when the strong taste
of the cheese proved unpalatable. Some idea of the
numbers involved can be gathered when, in 1592, it
was noted that there were 4,000 sheep in the Island.

To accommodate such interests buildings had
been erected. Known as wicks (hence the suffix to
South-, Further-, Knights-, etc), they were used as
dairies and as shelter for the shepherds. It is interesting to note that the word 'wick' has several
meanings: one authority defines it as a dairy farm in
one section and in another as a village or a marsh in
areas where salt was got by evaporation of water in
bays. *The Concise Oxford Dictionary of Current
English*, 5th edition, defines it as town, hamlet,
district. Although Canvey had its Red Hills they were
not, in the main, located in the wick areas.

I think it is reasonable to suppose that the
wicks were, in fact, dairy sheds established in the
areas and, although the modern fashion is to write

Knightswick Farm, c.1905

them as one word, e.g. Northwick, some earlier spellings show them as two, e.g. North wick, which supports my original contention.

The main snag for this rural industry was that Canvey, then a series of islets, could only be used when high tides did not cover all of the marshes. Some attempts had been made to wall in sections of the area against the incursions of the sea.* There are references to the separate construction of 154 perches of seawall in 1437 at a cost of 38 shillings and six-pence and, in 1438, making 80 perches at 13s.4d.† [A perch, standardised at 16½ feet could have varied between 9 and 26 feet]

This was not suitable for a growing and expanding industry and it was essential that the whole area be protected.

One must stop for a moment and consider the position. An island, used by the Romans to extract salt and as a port, has developed into a thriving agri-cultural area. To continue and develop it, some means had to be found to keep the sea at bay – such means was at hand. In modern times there are often a number of landowners without sufficient capital or technical expertise to utilise their holdings to the full: they form a consortium, negotiate terms with a finan-cial source who, for a consideration, make the utmost use of their land, employing the contractors and realising to the full what might otherwise be a wasted area.

Over 350 years ago that is exactly what happened at Canvey Island and a series of islands, some partly walled with a few buildings on them, used at various times for sheep pasture, became a unified whole.

Sir Roger Appleton's land at Canvey had passed to his son, Sir Henry, of Jarvis Hall, South Benfleet. In a deed (the document could have been prepared after

*Rough pile and wattle have been credited to the Trinovantes (a tribe from northern France and Belgium), 54 B.C. While this is an interesting theory and Canvey was in their territory, there is no evidence of their land reclamation.
† This was by the Manor of Southchurch, then owners of part of the Island.

some, if not all, of the work had been carried out) he, with others [Julius Sludder, John William and Mary Blackmore, Mr & Mrs Thomas Binckes and Abigail Baker], made an agreement by which one-third of the Island was given in fee simple* to the entrepreneur.

Dated 9th April, 1622, it was with Joas Croppen-burgh, described as a Dutch merchant, who would get his share for walling in 3,600 acres. Subsequent work followed which later made up for some of the land walled in, but which was 'thrown to the sea' because of 19th century flooding. However, he was offered a very sizeable landholding of "four hundred, three score and eleven acres and one hundred and twentie roode or thereabouts". On 1st December, 1623, Sir Henry passed over to Croppenburgh 471 acres, 120 rods.

It could not have been all straightforward for Philip Benton in his 19th century *The History of Rochford Hundred* (published in 58 parts between 1867 and 1888), says that Robert, the second Earl of Warwick, known as the Puritan Earl, was in 1626 "engaged in the reclamation of Canvey Island, and executed a deed wherein John Bucks of London engages to recover the Island (then consisting of 3,600 acres). The witnesses to his Lordship's signature were Richard Pulley, William Goughe, Richard Spittye, Jo. Attwood, John Brooke and others". Nothing more is known of this; it could have been an attempt by minor landowners to make a take-over bid.

The Dutch were, of course, masters of such reclamation work, as they had proved in their own country. Acting as agent, Croppenburgh employed such engineers as Cornelius Vermuden (later knighted by Charles I in 1628) and Cornelius Vandervanker. Croppen-burgh was commemorated by a canal on the Island and Vermuden by having a modern school named after him. Vandervanker seems almost wholly to have escaped recognition, although a property later in the Island's history had a name resembling an Anglicised version of his surname.

The lowland engineers were faced with a great

*Third Acre land lasted from 1623 to January, 1933, and mainly supported the upkeep of the sea wall. It was abolished by an Act of 1930.

Dutch cottage. Behind the pump is the Red Cow. c.1910

task, but one which they carried out superbly. Firstly, they had to build a barrier against the insidious tide and, having done so, their next task was to drain the Island.

The wall they erected survived - in the main - into the mid-20th century. Even in the East Coast Flood disaster of 1953 the barriers were not broken. The walls were over-topped by the water and the back of the walls was washed away, causing breaches. The structure that has now been constructed follows on their handiwork.

The original wall was built on a chalk foundation, of clay and faced with a sandy limestone, grey-green in colour, hard and resisting the sea - Kentish ragstone. It cost over £10,000. Properly maintained it was an impressive safeguard.

The drainage was a difficult job for the Island was (and still is) virtually flat. Dykes had to be cut to take the surface water from the fields and sluices provided through the wall to discharge the rainwater into the sea. Once again, the system that the Dutch used went on well into the present century and it is only in recent years that the Essex River Authority improved it.

The originators dug a delft ditch around the inner perimeter of the seawall, using the earth from that for the wall. From the arterial ditch ran subsidiary dykes. When they were brimming they shed their load into the fleets, which ran to the sluices. These endured and it was not until shortly before World War II that they were renewed. One that was originally installed was excavated in 1971. It gave many clues as to how the Dutch had reclaimed the land.

While the River Authority was providing its own system, it dug up Central Wall Road. This had long been believed to be an original Dutch seawall, superceded when Sixty Acres was walled in: the sluice discovery proved this. When they got 8 feet down workmen found what was first thought to be a coffin, they started clearing by hand and found a wooden pipe consisting of two elm-tree trunks, one 21 feet long and the other 10 feet, six inches in length. To construct this the Dutch had probably used a saw-pit, in the same way as wooden battleships were later built. Adzes had been used to hollow them out. Once this was done the sawn-off part was replaced, 'nailed' with wooden pins.

Its use was proved by a lip to provide a flap to prevent the sea coming in at high tide. This sluice was between 24 and 30 inches in diameter on the outside. The bore was 16 inches wide by 11 inches deep.

Appropriately, the pipe is now preserved in the grounds of the Dutch Cottage Museum; this building is at Hill Hall and was built in 1618. It is octagonal in shape and is believed to have been used by the Dutch workmen when they built the seawall. It has a conical thatched roof. Such cottages may have been specially designed for this part of the country. Although this is smaller than those on the mainland, they are completely unknown to many people from Holland who have visited them. There is another in Canvey Village, dated 1621. The museum, of two storeys, is plastered, timber framed and brick. It was opened in 1962 by M. Van Ekelen of the Dutch Embassy in London, having been given to Canvey Council by the trustees of the A M Clark estate. It has had a varied history. In addition to surviving two world wars and the 1953 flood, it was at one time a labourer's cottage for Hill Hall Farm, which had been built two years earlier in 1616 and was demolished in 1932. Later it became a school where sewing, sums and reading were taught at four (old) pence a week. At least one of its pupils came from Benfleet. Later a residence, it was from 1925 to 1929 the week-end home of a London doctor.

It was not only turning marshes into an island at which the Dutch excelled. They also brought religion to Canvey. In 1628 200 Dutch workers petitioned the King to allow them to worship in their own language. This was agreed, the service and minister were to conform to the Dutch Church in London.

A wooden chapel was built and the Dutch elected their first pastor, Cornelius Jacobsen, who became "Minister of the Divine Word in England in the Netherlandish community at Canvey Island". On 16th

Dutch cottage and Red Cow, c.1930

December, 1645, Adriaen Munnic became Ecclesiaste.

However, English residents on Canvey who went to church at St Mary the Virgin's at Benfleet thought it would be a good idea if they could sometimes use the Dutch church: this was refused. On Whit Monday, 1656, the local English residents marched to the church and demanded the keys of the Dutch building. The Dutch refused and the English retired, defeated in the clash that followed.

On 14th October, 1704, the last named Island Dutch Minister, Dom Emilius Von Cuilenborg, was buried at Benfleet. After that the Dutch appeared to go and for the next few years it would seem that the Island was looked after from the mainland.

There is a well-documented case of psychic phenomena during that period. In a house occupied by Jan Smagges, a farmer, a series of incidents happened on 10, 13, 14 and 16 September, 1709. They took the form of the breaking of windows, apparitions, noises and the killing of a chicken. A person described as an English curate, Mr Lord, was able to drive away the spirit. It has been suggested that these happenings were a ruse, so that contraband could be removed from the church or that it was an elaborate hoax, as there is no other reference to a Canvey curate. I think that the smuggling theory can be discounted. Such happenings would draw attention to, rather than away from, the Island. As for the point about no other references to a curate, I have discovered that in 1704 James Lord was parish clerk at Benfleet and could have been in Holy Orders and might thus be described as the curate. The incident is fully described in a pamphlet of 28 pages in a letter from Maldon to a 'gentleman in London' and was published in the year of the incident described.

An English church, dedicated to St Katherine, Virgin and Martyr, was built and consecrated on 11th June, 1712, by the Bishop of London. This was replaced in 1745 by another church, dedicated to St Peter, Apostle and Martyr. It was provided by Daniel Scratton of Prittlewell and by local donations. Scratton gave £10 a year for church services and an additional £10 per annum for a minister to preach sermons there

20 times a year. When these took place in the tim-
bered, red-tile-roofed building a flag was run up on a
staff at the west end. Even up to the mid-1880s the
flagstaff survived.

Seamen were buried on Canvey and on 21
August, 1806, Francois Pierre of the *Eurides* from Sur
inham was interred.

A third church was built in 1875 and consecrated on 9th November of that year by the Bishop
of Rochester. The porch and some of the windows
were used from a previous building. The bell was cast
in 1875. Civil and ecclesiastical rights were obtained in
1881. The parish church, as it then was, was replaced
by one dedicated to St Nicholas on another site, in
Long Road, in 1960.

It has always been generally supposed that the
former parish church was built on the site of the
Dutch chapel. However, this may not be so. The diary
of London barrister, Arthur Munby, for Tuesday, 14
February, 1860, notes a petition received to convert a
Dutch chapel at Canvey into a church and notes that
the last curate (on £40 a year) died of want of money
to buy food. This would suggest that the Dutch
building in fact survived their departure. Maps do show
the Dutch structure, but are not sufficiently detailed
to suggest its exact location.

But Canvey had earlier seen the Dutch in another guise. During the second war with them, they
raided the Medway, burning British warships and, in
June, 1667, a squadron blockaded the Thames, near
Canvey.

It was at first light on 9th June that Lieutenant
-Admiral Willem Joseph Van Ghent, in charge of
Dutch frigates, turned towards the mouth of the river.
In the evening it was calm and he anchored off Hole
Haven. The tide turned and a party of men landed on
the Island. Their raid was against the orders of
Admiral Michiel Adriaanzoon de Ruyter (1607-76),
commander of the Dutch fleet. For the damage they
caused they were later punished.

Contemporary accounts tell of the burning of a
house, the destruction of 8 houses, the burning of
barns, the theft of small boats and plunder. They took

St Nicholas

fresh meat on the hoof (sheep) from Canvey.

We, in our more sophisticated age, when the slain have to be counted in their thousands and guide-book towns reduced to rubble before we are inter-ested, would think this of little significance. To an area with a small resident population devoted to agri-culture and few homesteads, it was vastly different. There had been the sullen roar of cannon fire (heard in London) and then the arrival of the marauders.

Their boats grounded on the stone-faced sea-wall, near the 'Lobster Smack' and a fighting force surged over. No military strength was available to give battle: other sources refer to the Essex Militia mobil-ised at Leigh. The residents cowered in their homes as the rampage went on. There was only one thing to be done: the alarm must be raised.

At the start of a long summer day, riders raced through the Canvey-Benfleet ford. Then they flogged their tired beasts down cart-track roads to the largest town, Chelmsford, raising the alarm through the villages and hamlets on the way.

From Chelmsford Sir John Bramston wrote to London "The enemie hath burnt barns and a house at Canvie". Sir Henry Appleton was more specific to the Secretary of State. He put quill to parchment to say "The Dutch have landed at Canvey and plundered it to the extent of eight inconsiderable houses, they have also taken several small boats".

The Government showed themselves less than resolute and prepared to move from London while the Dutch sail was off the Island.

I was puzzled by the reference to Sir John Bramston, but discovered that he was appointed Vice-Admiral of Essex in 1661 until about 1680 and as Deputy Lieutenant in 1662 and 1676.

No previous reference has been made to the feelings of the Dutch settlers on the Island when their compatriots landed, but evidence has come to light that there was a potential fifth columnist among them, albeit unsuccessful. Allegations had been made that a boat from Leigh told the Dutch of movements by British fireboats and a series of investigations took place, but that particular charge was unfounded.

However, at an examination at Rochford John Cole and his wife, Rosamund, and Thomas Jannings (described as a husbandman) said that John Gentbridge waved his hat to a Dutch boat to take him away. It would seem that the man was from the Island. He was not rescued, as he signed his examination Jan of Gentbrijg. It would appear that this incident took place after the actual landing on the Island.

One correction must be made concerning the raid. In some history books it is recorded that the raiders burnt the church. This, of course, is not true.

A landowner who did suffer was the Rev George Maul, rector of Vange. In his will of 23rd September, 1667, he decreed "that after other bequests I give the residue of my goods, chattels, plate to be sold and the proceeds to get funds for the repair and rebuilding of my house and barn, lately burned down by the Dutch on Canvey Island".

So ended the second Dutch occupation, far less fruitful than the first. A footnote in a history book which, for the first time, brought Canvey to the attention of the outer world.

Despite the alarms and excursions the area remained unfrequented and John Ogilby's massive volume *Road Maps of England and Wales* published in 1675, ignored it. Morden's map (c.1700) showed the Island walled in, with one building, 'The Chappel'. However, Ogilby's lapse was made good by Emanual Bowen who, in 1720, provided *Britannia Depicta or Ogilby Improved:* mistakes were rectified and, in the map, Canvey is firmly shown in its right place.

In 1722 Muilman's *History of Essex* Scar House is noted as a farm and this survived, although empty, until 1940. A section of the seawall has preserved the name Scar's Elbow to modern times.

That great journalist, Daniel Defoe, has an interesting account of local conditions in his *Tour of the Eastern Counties* first published in 1724. Much doubt has been cast on certain of his observations and I shall deal with them later.

First of all he refers to the area as 'Candy Island' and I have confirmed his use of it with other contemporary records. He says that generally in the

Thameside area he frequently met men with five, six, 14, 15 or even more wives. Happily, he does not conclude that this is an example of (south) eastern harems. His explanation is that natives of the district, who were immune from the traditional local disease of ague, went into the 'uplands' (the hilly mainland) for a succession of brides. The young wives died after six months to a year and were replaced, successively.

Defoe speaks of a farmer who had had 25 wives and of his 35-year-old son, who had had 15. He realised that, although in some cases the final figure might be exaggerated, some truth lay behind it. He also points out that the local residents were not, in the main, old. More than half of those living there had come from other parts for the advantage of good farms.

Defoe has been derided by some people who have doubted the accuracy of his facts. While, like he, I do not go along with the ultimate totals, I believe that there is a general basis of truth. Researchers have established that the large numbers of burials involved are not recorded either locally or in the records of the parishes of which the Island then formed part. It must be remembered that in those days people were not so particular about such things and it might well be that the unfortunate brides were interred in unmarked graves elsewhere.

A close study of Defoe's tour shows that, in other instances, he dealt with the minutiae; for example, in his account of the siege of Colchester he gives the number of those who surrendered as 3,526 and gives the ranks of all of them.

Ague (or intermittent fever) was endemic in all marshland areas. Sufferers were advised to avoid bad air or stagnant pools, but, owing to the terrain, this was impossible. Even medical reference books in the early part of this century still dealt with it, quoting quinine as a preventative and curative. This first made its appearance in Western Europe in 1640, but it was to be many years before its use was recognised in the lowlands of Essex.

A survey book (1741-89) shows the district carrying on in a quiet, industrious manner. Items from the Canvey Surveyor's Book of 1742 shows the work being carried out at that time. On 14th May a day's work for a cart, three horses and two men cost 6s.6d. On 5th July two days' work was needed to heighten the road at the causeway. Two carts, four horses and three men were employed at a total cost of £1. Six fagots were used to block a hole in the causeway at a cost of 4s.

But it was not all work and no play: an unspecified number of men received drink - to the value of one shilling.

Another item deserves quoting in its entirety -

"For a new foot Bridge over the Creek into the Island £14.13s.8d."

This would be an actual wood-bridge running over the Creek enabling the rare coaches and foot-passengers to cross dry shod just before low tide.

It was not until about 1830 that Canvey received a better access. Originally the entrance was over Benfleet Downs. The road was diverted through Benfleet itself on application to the Court of Quarter Sessions. The lack of a proper bridge meant that Canvey would remain a very rural community, cut off from mainland amenities.

Thomas Archer (1750-1832) was curate at Canvey, North Benfleet and Rawreth. To preach at all he had to gallop from parish to parish, reciting benediction as he dashed down the church aisle. Before his congregation had risen from their knees he was off and away on horseback to his next service.

On 28th September, 1770, a stranger was reported 'drownded' coming out of the Island. There is no evidence to show what the person was doing. The only presumption that can be made is that he was a tramp or vagrant.

An anecdote survives from the time the first Vicar of Canvey was appointed. He was told "We never buried no one here till you came, except them as was drownded" The use of the word 'drownded' thus survived over a hundred years.

Burials did take place during the period - at nearby Benfleet.

Despite the stout seawalls Canvey was flooded* in 1731 and again on 16th February, 1736. Caused by a north-west gale at full moon, it was the highest tide for 135 years and drowned all the cattle.

In 1790 the matter was taken to Parliament, as there were no proper means to keep the wall in a good state. Meanwhile, Canvey was flooded in the spring of 1791 and in the winter of that year[x]. However, in 1792 an Act of Parliament (32 Geo.III Cap.31) vested sea wall maintenance in a Board of Commissioners[t]. Under this Act the Canvey Island Commission was established, their first meeting being at the "Anchor" public house, Benfleet on Wednesday, 9th May, 1792.

Although they were empowered to rate not only the land granted to the Dutch (the Third Acre Land), but also to levy charges on other land if Third Acre revenue was insufficient, they did not do so to an extent that would help. A 19th century Act empowered the Commission to rate free land and raise a loan to pay for damage done.

In 1793 James Asser's map showed the Island's circumference as 13¾ miles; total free land was 2,257 acres, 3 roods, 30 poles. The Third Acre portion (referred to as "Dutch charity") consisted of 776 acres, 3 roods, 17 poles. The church yard totalled 23 poles.

By and large the French wars left the Island untouched. This was because it was considered unsuitable for a landing 'for if they did they never could march out to form and fight us' commented Colonel George Hanger in 1804 in *Reflections on the menaced invasion*. There was still the dreaded press gang, as witness the experience of a Leigh man.

He had been pressed (taken by the press gang) and, at the time of the great naval mutiny at the Nore in 1797, he had escaped. He tried to reach home, "but the tide drifted me up to Canvey Island

*First Essex flooding recorded was in 31 A.D.

x Wall damage of 2 February, 1791, £476.1s.0d; 26/27 November, £65.6s.0d.

t"An Act for more effectively embanking, draining and otherwise improving the Island of Canvey in the county of Essex".

and there I got ashore". Pursued, he dodged his would-
be captors and "the third day I saw them go back. All
this time I lived on corn and dirty ditchwater".

The 1823 edition of *The Steam Boat Companion*
contains a fascinating description of Canvey, presenting
an enchanting rural scene.

It says, "Within the mouth of the Thames, and
separated from the main land, which is Essex, by a
narrow, irregular, winding swale [creek], interspersed
with small patches of verdure, and is about five miles
from east to west, and about four from north to
south, in many places well cultivated, and produces,
besides other pulse [edible seeds of peas, beans and
lentils] excellent beans, vetches [plant of the pea
family], &c., the greater part of it is the property of
William Calcraft, Esq., M.P.* In the centre is a lake
near one mile over, affording in the winter rare
amusement for the sportsmen for the wild ducks,
which delight at that season in inland waters, are to
be found there in abundance. In spring and summer the
Aurelian [collector of insects] may pursue his pleasure
to the highest advantage, for the border of the pool is
fimbriated [literally, bordered with hairs] with a great
variety of flowers and these are the attraction for an
immense variety of insects, some of which are so full
of beautiful colours as hardly to be equalled in
Europe. Towards the north end of the Island stands in
an obscure situation, an old stone chapel, with one
bell, the lodge that contains this melancholy monitor
projects from the top of the main building, and is only
large enough to contain its solitary inmate; f om this
bell falls a rope on the outside to accommodate the
ringer, exposed to the observation of the passer by,
which being once cut off as high as a man could
reach, the parishioners could only be prevailed on to
supply the deficiency with a hayband; a wanton cow
beheld the tempting bait, and preferred the twisted

*On enquiry at the Research Division of the Home and Parlia-
mentary Affairs Section of the House of Commons Library, I was
informed that "No one of the name of William Calcraft was an
M.P. between 1705 and 1885". However, William Calcraft (1800-
79) was Common Hangman of London from 1829 to 1874!

prize to her own luxuriant pasture, sacrilegiously devoured the new bell rope to the highest extent of her ability, and to the great chagrin of the clerk, who was now divested of the means of calling his neighbours together, and of the gratification of clerical benediction.

"At the western end of the island is a creek of great utility to the fishermen in all weathers, called Hole-Haven, which affords not only shelter, but good anchorage, from the western extremity round to Canvey Point."

In 1848, when the Island was part of the Barstable Hundred* it was said to have 277 inhabitants and about 3,600 acres of rich grazing land for cattle and sheep. It was then about 6 miles long, which included the Point, at the eastern end of the Island.

At that time there was a raised causeway across Benfleet Creek. The church was St Peter, although Canvey was still a part of Prittlewell, the rectorial tithes being sold by Daniel, Earl of Nottingham, to Mr Scratton of Billericay, later belonging to a descendant of his, D R Scratton.

The benefice was a perpetual curacy, valued at £58, in the patronage of the Bishop of London, the incumbent being the Rev William Ray, B.C.L., curate of Eastwood. Canvey tithes in Prittlewell were apportioned by agreement in 1839. Estimated acreage was 616 and they were commuted for £190 a year. Land owners were Jonathan Wood, George Bullas, John Alliston, William Hilton, Emma Kerr, the Rev Roland Berkeley and Charles Berkeley.

In 1848 landowners included Spitty (preserved in the name of Spitty Estate), Ballie and Curtis; licensee of the 'Lobster Smack' was Crisp Molyneux Harridge; John Hunt was the only listed shopkeeper. The nearest post office was at Benfleet, where letters were despatched at Simeon Daine's at 2.30, via Rochford. Benfleet artisans included Charles Andrew, blacksmith; Edward Blakeley, shoemaker; Thomas Blakeley, wheel-

*Barstable Hundred extended about 14 miles along the north bank of the Thames from Gravesend Reach and Tilbury Fort to Canvey. The Hundred was in the Southern Parliamentary division of Essex and in the Brentwood Police Division.

The Lobster Smack, c.1920

wright; James Garrad, shoemaker; Daniel Mansfield, shoemaker; and John Wood and Abraham Moor, carriers, who went to Chelmsford on Fridays. These tradesmen must have known the Islanders well. For education the nearest school to Canvey was Miss C E Sopwith's boarding establishment at Rose Cottage. The nearest wharf, too, was at Benfleet, run by William Howard. Barge owners included Mary Ann Howard. There were a number of farmers and, of course, the village (population in 1841 707) had its own Vicar, the Rev H R Lloyd, M.A., who presided over the 'handsome and stately structure' of St Mary's. It was described as having a nave, side aisles, chancels, and 'a stone tower containing five bells and crowned by a lofty wooden spire'. The vicarage had been valued in 1831 at £225.

I have dwelt at length with Benfleet, as it was the nearest place to the Island. Residents would deal there with matter of importance and, of course, passed through on their way to the county town.

Canvey's population figures are hard to arrive at or to justify. Both in 1841 and 1848 the number of inhabitants was given as 277. In 1866 it had apparently dropped to 111 and risen again to 282 in 1887. Unfortunately Philip Benton in his monumental *Rochford Hundred* merely notes that in 1867 of Benfleet's population in 1861, 31 lived on Canvey. I am inclined to take this lower figure as being accurate for the period. My own theory for the various discrepancies is that, with Canvey divided between mainland parishes, their returns were not all that could be desired.

I received additional confirmation of this when I contacted the Office of Population Censuses and Surveys for Canvey's population as recorded in the 1851 Census Returns. I was told "Unfortunately the population of Canvey Island was included in various parishes so it is impossible to give you the information you require". The Census for that period had been most detailed in other respects and exact ages, as well as birthplaces, were given.

Therefore the so-called mystery of the rising and falling inhabitants' number was based on a fallacy. It is likely that, until past the middle of the 19th century, the number of residents did not exceed two figures and the then number of permanent structures would give further credence to this.

The great Essex historian Philip Benton had quite a lot to say about Canvey. He first reviewed the location and vital statistics of the district, noted Roman pottery found at the eastern end of the Island and also paid attention to the earlier walls prior to the work carried out through Sir Henry Appleton. Dealing with subsequent flooding he noted "The highest ground is near the chapel where stock used to be driven when in danger". It is recalled that the 1953 flood ebbed from that point.

The noted writer had much to say of the then modern drainage. He said: "The Island was much improved through the exertions and example of the late Mr Hilton, of Danbury, which were the means of recovering 10 acres in every hundred from the waste [inferior land used communally]; the gutters and sluices being laid from four to six feet lower than they were 70 years ago.

"The salubrity of the Island is much improved owing to this and the artesian wells, of which there are about seven, which average about 250 feet in depth, the water from all occasionally flowing over the surface*. The water at Charles Asplin's farm, called Brick House, is conveyed in iron pipes to several of the grazing marshes, the flow of water being regulated by stop cocks; in one instance it is conveyed 80 rods, and the system well merits an inspection".

Benton is particularly good on the ownership of the island. At that time, it will be recalled, the Island was administered by mainland parishes. He relentlessly traced land ownership back to the 16th century. He says "The most ancient possessor of lands here upon record, was Edward Baker, Esq., who in 1543 held under Nicolas Wentworth several marshes. In 1557 Sir Roger Appleton, knight, held lands and likewise his great grandson, Henry Appleton, Esq., in 1604. In fact, nearly the whole Island, called 'Candy', alias Canvey, belonged to the Appletons, together with the feedings, fishing, and water courses surrounding it (cum omnibus

*In the early 1900s one was still in use at Leigh Beck Farm.

juribus). Shorman or Sporman marsh belonging to the last named was formerly the property of one Latham, gentleman. Sir Henry, the encloser, has already been mentioned. The daughters of William Lukyn possessed two salt marshes, held of the honour* of Rayleigh called Langdowne Wyck and Lynward, and paid yearly a quit rent† of 2s. and 2d. This was in the reign of Elizabeth.

"'Antletts', otherwise 'Antleach' [corrupted in living memory to 'Antlers'] (called Brick House), and Sauldry marshes lying in Pitsea and South Benfleet were owned by John Fell in 1749. One of this family sold the property to Major General Sir James Charles Dalbiac, K.C.B., who resold it to Jonathan Wood. Upon the latter gentleman's death in 1860, it was sold by the trustees under the will, and bought by Charles Asplin, of Tilbury Place. Upon this farm is a marsh called Gay Marsh from the prevalence of Lathyrus Tuberosus a plant which it seems impossible to eradicate. It has a flower like an everlasting pea, with a bulb at the root, which is edible, and is said to have been introduced by the Dutch.

"'Southwick Marsh' otherwise 'Tree Farm', in the parish of North Benfleet, was formerly the property of Col. Wm Brewse Kersteman; it was purchased by Jonathan Wood, and being sold by his trustees under his will, was bought by H N Wood (testator's son).

"'Little Brick House', in North Benfleet and Prittlewell, purchased likewise by Mr Wood, of the Colonel, was sold by his trustees, and bought by William Kynaston of Gresham Street, London. Col. William Brewse Kersteman, said to have been of Somersetshire, but who resided at one time in Devonshire, and married at Colchester, was a collateral relation of Colonel Kersteman, of Loftmans. His mother was a Miss Brewse.

"'Fatherwick' and 'Chafflets' were formerly the

*A grouping of several knights' fees (an area held by a knight), lordships or manors under a lord and honorial court.

† It was a fixed rent paid by free and copy (a tenure dependent upon custom and the lord's will, abolished in 1926) holders of a manor in discharge of other services.

Small Gaines

property of James Holbrook of Tottenham and afterwards of his sister, Mrs Wakelin of Tottenham [a grand dame who, when nearly 80, went up Vesuvius and travelled through Italy and Germany in her carriage].

"They were long in the Wood family as lessees; the latter for about a century. They belong now to Alfred and Charles Layard. The house and buildings upon Chaffletts were consumed by fire about 80 years ago, during its occupation by the Wood family.

"'Russell's' and other marshlands adjoining were purchased by Henry Wood (father of the above-named Jonathan Wood) of Colonel W Brewse Kersteman.

"The 'Waterside' farm, part of Hadleigh and the rest, together with the House, in South Benfleet, belongs to the Dean and Chapter of St Paul's; William Hilton, of Danbury, was formerly lessee, and it is now in the tenure of his son, George Hilton of Flemings, in Runwell. Henry Wood occupied it about 60 years ago, and suring his tenancy a fire consumed everything but the house. Being uninsured, his neighbours subscribed most liberally to mitigate his loss; and, to his honour be it said, he afterwards insisted uopn restoration when fortune again smiled upon him."

The stilted words of those times illustrate to the full the Island nature (and one that still survives to this very day, for I have personal knowledge of two incidents where funds have been launched locally when properties have been destroyed). A closely-knit community looking after its own and repaying, as a matter of course, a debt of honour in full.

"'Knight's Wick', situated in North Benfleet and Hadleigh, formerly the property of William Hilton of Danbury, is now owned by his descendants.

"'Monk's Wick' is owned by the Dean and Chapter of St Paul's, George Hilton is lessee. It is situated in South Benfleet.

"'Small Gains', in Hadleigh and Prittlewell, comprises what is called in old deeds 'Low Marsh', with the addition of land bought of Richard Harrison. It is owned by Daniel Nash.

"'Sluice' farm, partly in South Benfleet, belongs to J A Nash of Berkshire.

Northwick

"'Hill Hall' farm in the parish of Laindon, is situated near the chapel. It formerly was Thirlwall's successor to Powley, rector of Bower's Gifford.

"'Dutch Church' farm, all grass, in Laindon and North Benfleet, belongs to Henry New.

"'Pantile' belongs to E Woodward of Billericay and likewise 'Kersey', situate in South Benfleet. He purchased these farms of King's College, Cambridge; they were formerly parcel of Kersey Priory at Hadleigh in Suffolk [I believe that the 'Kersey Farm' referred to was literally in South Benfleet, as there is still a farm in that area with that name].

"'Kibcaps', 'Lovens', 'Scar House' and 'North Wick' belong to the Hilton family. Major Spitty at that time owned 'The Sixty Acres Farm'."

The roll continues that 'Leigh Beck' farm was formerly the property of Henry Comyns Berkeley of Lincoln's Inn Fields, from whom it was bought by Henry Wood of Hadleigh Park. 'Chimnies' [later corrupted to 'Chimneys'] in Bowers Gifford was also Hilton owned. 'Rack Hall', or 'Wreck Hall', otherwise 'Southchurch Marsh' at the south-east of the Island, of about 40 acres, was all third-acre land. The original purchase price was 100 guineas by Ralph Robinson of Horndon in about 1770.

How inflation reared its ugly head is shown in the following anecdote - "This was resold in 1815 at the Bell Inn, Horndon-on-the-Hill, by William Jeffries to the grandfather of the present proprietor, Daniel Nash, for £1300. The family had made up their minds to let it go for £800 [presumably because of the war with the French, farm land had increased in value - an increase of nearly £700 in 45 years was not too bad!], but the company being stimulated by a copious circulation of sherry, and a competition springing up between Nash and Wilson of Rochford Hall, the result was as above stated."

In these days of muggers it is interesting to note that "When the purchase money was paid at the Lion Inn, Rayleigh [then kept by Witham] to Jeffries and Charles Robinson (now of Horndon) it was deposited in the boots of the recipients, for fear of footpads".

The farm was named 'Wreck Hall' because Ralph Robinson bought from the underwriters the wreck of the *Ajax*, which had been driven ashore opposite South Shoebury, the timbers being used for the farm. [Again, the name survives in 'Wreckhall Court', accommodation for elderly and other people in Gafzelle Drive, administered by Castle Point District Council.]

At that time the soil was heavy, but was good for corn. Arable portions were laid up in beds from 3 to 4 rods in width. Road repairs were carried out through the different parishes and were described as excellent. A most important post at that time was that of marsh bailiff and it had been in the Wellard family for 72 years. The bailiff worked under the direction of the Sea Wall Commissioners.

Reference is made to an interesting series of law suits. Brown mustard was grown with cereals (an earlier note had been made to their being a valuable part of the Island's economy). The unnamed grower claimed the right of rubbing the mustard out of the tithe trave; he won, but while it was in progress of settlement, the stacks rotted.

Benton's chapter on Canvey concludes with the dry (and I use the word advisedly) comment, "The Island 70 years ago was a noted place for smuggling".

I have dealt with this at length as it throws up some interesting subjects. First of all, there are no references to subjects that might have excited his pen - the 'Lobster Smack' inn and the Dutch cottages are not mentioned. Presumably the ferry was not of so much note, as the creek would mostly be forded at low tide. Again, there is no suggestion of summer visitors.

The land holdings he does deal with are, of course, of paramount importance and we must be grateful to him; however, one must be guarded to some extent.

Let us consider the agricultural situation as it then existed. The Island had been reclaimed from tidal sheep pastures in the mid-17th century. 200 years afterwards it had changed substantially to arable farming. Throughout the 19th century there are con-

stant references to cereal crops. A so-called farmers'
prayer of the period suggested that he called for 'a
wet winter (to make his crops grow) and a bloody war
(to increase the demand)'. The earlier-related anecdote of the land sold in 1815 shows its importance.
Although the selling price had been increased arti-
ficially, the margin of profit, even on the envisaged
selling price, was substantial.

Land ownership had widened and set a pattern
that has steadily gone on. It became the property of
people both near and far. One of the was Major
Thomas Jenner Spitty of Billericay, whose relations had
an even earlier connection with the Island. His grand-
mother was Elizabeth (nee Innott) of Shoreham,
Sussex, and her father at one time lived at Leigh Beck
Farm.

Major Spitty, who died on 26th January, 1898,
at Billericay, aged 86, was commissioned in the East
Essex Militia, being appointed Captain in 1834 and 20
years later a Major commanding the Essex Rifles, then
stationed at the Tower of London: when it was later
stationed at Windsor, he was presented to Queen
Victoria. Appointed a Justice of the Peace in April,
1839, he became a Deputy Lieutenant of the County
and, in 1881, High Sheriff. A regular attender at the
Court of Quarter Sessions, he was Finance Committee
Chairman. He was also Billericay Bench Chairman and,
at the time of his death, was the oldest and senior
J.P.

A keen sportsman, he drove tandem and kept a
pack of beagles. A fair shot, his wildfowl shooting was
at nearby Bowers Gifford (formerly Bowers-le-
Gifford), overlooking the western end of the Island.

Agriculture fell on hard times during the latter
years of his life. Particularly bleak was 1878 and he
granted tenants a 10% remission, later extended to 40
or 45%. A most generous gesture on his part and one
that, at the time of his death, attracted tribute to
'his highest integrity of character... and above all an
unostentatious liberality'. He was described as a
Liberal Unionist in politics, although (probably as a
soldier) not taking an active part.

Buccleuch Lodge, Leigh Beck, c.1905. Marla, Arly, Duport, Vickers, Hopkinson & Tubby Leslie Bugler are the boys in the picture

Meanwhile, the Island's agricultural life had continued its even tenor, enlivened by an annual fair for the sale of toys, ribbons, gingerbread, fruits and the like, outside the 'Lobster Smack'. It took place on 25th June and was well established by 1767. It was one of 43 recorded in Essex in Owen's *New Book of Fairs* and was still in full operation in 1848. However, when the Government in 1889 published its two volume *Market Rights and Tolls* it was no longer shown, along with many others. At South Benfleet the fair was on 24th August and at Hadleigh the day before Canvey.

On 22nd September, 1857, at Canvey Island, Ben Court (Champion, 1838-45), aged 42, met Nat Langham, aged 37, in a 60 round grudge fight, which came about through a family feud and, although Langham had been down 59 times, he was still standing in the 60th round. They decided to shake hands and make up the quarrel.

Tom Sayers - they called him the greatest Champion of all - made a habit of battling on the Island. He drew with Aaron Jones on 19th February, 1857, after an epic contest. Some say it lasted 62 rounds, other 65, when it got dark and the referee ruled a draw.

But there was no dispute over the return bout. Sayers won, in the 85th round, when his opponent's seconds threw in the towel.

Sayers was quicker in a Championship fight on 16th June, 1858, perhaps because, in addition to the purse, there was a handsome side-stake of 300 sovereigns. He beat Tom Paddock in 21 rounds. To show his sporting nature, he collected £30 from among the spectators for his defeated opponent.

Employment at Canvey was still agricultural and there was a thriving 'export' of hay. Crops were loaded on to barges and it has often been said that Derby winners ate their way to fame and fortune on local grass that had been dried for fodder.

Some farms had their own wharves for this purpose. A map of Leigh Beck Farm of 1869 shows a wharf on the southern sea wall. Within living memory there was a similar situation at Thorney Bay. Here, the wall had been cut and a wooden, locked gate let in; this, when open, led to a stone embankment on one of the arms of the bay. Cart loads of the precious crops could then be loaded at high tide.

In 1870-1 Canvey was thought to have another use. The Metropolis Sewage and Essex Reclamation Company, whose aim was to collect sewage from the end of the Northern Outfall Sewer and take it elsewhere, came into the picture. The last of their three plans was to take the sewage by conduit to a part of Canvey's shore. It did not reach fruition – if that is the right word!

A fascinating picture of Canvey comes from Dickens' *Dictionary of the Thames (from Oxford to the Nore)* of 1880.

"Canvey is situated on the Thames, about 12 miles below Gravesend, and is close to Hole Haven or Holy Haven and not far from Thames Haven.

"There is a comfortable and unobtrusive inn, where boating men are frequently accommodated with bed and board [The 'Lobster Smack'].

"The population of the Island, purely agricultural is about 300. There is a very pretty little church, dedicated to St Katharine, with services on Sunday at 11 and 3, and sometimes at 6.30 also [I love the use of the word 'sometimes'!].

"Holy Communion is celebrated on the first Sunday at noon, and on the third at 8.30 a.m.; the service is choral.

"Smuggling still continued and this part of the Essex coast has a history of runs carried out by the 'gentlemen'.

"There is a coastguard station on the Island, and Benfleet Station is on the land side about three miles from the water."

Then comes the first published plug for Canvey as a seaside resort – "There is a fine shell bay and beach, which nearly at all times of the tide is a most pleasant walk close to the sea.

"Nearest railway station, Benfleet, on the London, Tilbury, and Southend Railway, about one hour 30 minutes from London. Railway fares to London, 1st 3s.9d, 6s.3d.; 2nd, 2s.10d, 4s.9d; 3rd, 1s.11d, 3s.10d."

Coastguard Station, Holehaven, Canvey

Coastguard Station, c.1908. The Kynoch Hotel can just be seen to the right of the building.

The strength of the coastguard station at Hole Haven was Chief Officer, a chief boatman, two commissioned boatmen and four boatmen.

One can imagine the Island of that time like a green-walled park, the boundaries of the seawall enclosing the district from the sea. There were great fields of ripening corn, said to be the finest in the country. In 1887 there was 'very rich grazing and some arable land'. A small population amply catered for in its religious needs by the quiet, tree-girt church.

Marvellous dawns, a hint of their past grandeur can sometimes be seen even today. Great flaming sunsets that have forever been enshrined on canvas by artists*.

Brooding over all, the often mist-shrouded sentinel hills of Benfleet and Kent. The only persistent sounds that of the gulls; sometimes a corncrake or a heron would be in attendance. Communications were sketchy; South Benfleet had one mail to London and received two daily in 1879.

On 18th January, 1881, there was severe flooding and land was lost, a total of 1,200 acres being submerged. Walls on the south-east side of the Island for over 3 miles were affected. In some places the top was carried away completely and the whole island was in danger of being flooded by the next tide.

So serious was this attack that the Committee of Management met and applied to Chatham military authorities for military labour. They came from the School of Military Engineering, one source states. However, it is more probable that the personnel were from one of the service companies of the Royal Engineers stationed in the Chatham area, under the overall command of the Commandant, School of Military Engineering. At that time the units there were the 3rd, 7th, 8th, 11th and one section of the 23rd companies. The Commanding Officer, Royal Engineers, HQ Eastern District, Colchester, would have

*John Constable's 'Hadleigh Castle', oils on canvas, shows Canvey in the background. The painting is at the Tate Gallery, London. It is from a pencil sketch made in the summer of 1814. It was exhibited at the Royal Academy in 1829.

Road to Leigh Beck, c.1920

possibly been instrumental in recommending R E
assistance.

This would have been useful training for them in
connection with one of their responsibilities – maintenance of the seaward defences at major naval bases
and coastal battery positions. Lt.Col. J E South,
Librarian of the Royal Engineers Corps, Chatham, has
researched the information and says that there was a
large amount of coastal erosion work undertaken by
them. Responsibility for military works service was
handed over from the R Es to the Department of the
Environment (PSA) in 1959.

The Engineers were augmented by between 100
and 200 men from a London firm of engineers. About
130 men were also engaged by the Committee as local
labour at 4s.6d. a day.

The damage stretched right along the seaward
face of the wall from Scar House to Leigh Beck
Farm. To combat it the largest labour force since the
Dutch left was mobilised to deal with it under wintry
conditions, using what would seem to us primitive
methods. Apart from the manual work involved, there
were the logistics of the situation – the quartering of
the men, their provisioning, even sanitation.

The nearest railway station was at Benfleet.
Equipment, materials, all had to wait until they could
be fetched across at low tide or floated in or barged
over. To the furthest point it was over 4 miles.

It was later in the decade, 28th July, 1883, that
the Commission held their first meeting under the
Canvey Island Sea Defences Act, 1883.

It was in the mid-1880s* that Canvey's attractions as a holiday resort were put to an even wider
public. A booklet called *New Holidays in Essex* with a
cover illustrating Hadleigh Castle [known as the Tower
of Essex during the Wars of the Roses], with Canvey
in the background, came out. Its drawings include a
Canvey Dutch cottage and a view of the 'Lobster

*In 1879 steamboats could be hired to take 500 passengers from
Westminster to Southend for £60 on Mondays and Saturdays or £55
for any day except Saturday, Sunday or Monday. This was for
private excursion parties. The 3rd class return railway fare
(Great Eastern) was 4/-.

The Point Colony

Smack' (then under a different name) from the river.

After reviewing the Dutch wall-building, it described the cottages as 'tiny octagonal cottages about 11 feet high and broad, with brick foundations and a superstructure of mud, kept in position by a pargetting of cockle shells'.

"There is a good beach for bathing near Deadman's Point; fishing and boating can be freely had, wildfowling is a winter attraction."

A further description is evocative of the wild marsh-fringed seaboard - "There is a fine view from the lofty, sturdy sea-wall. Up stream the Thames looks like a land-locked bay; below it widens to the sea. As the clouds hurry by, driven by the fresh breezes that blow up or down the channel between the Essex and Kentish hills, throwing up the ruins of Hadleigh at times as on a lantern screen."

But there was a grimmer side to Canvey, for in 1891 powder hulks, each in charge of a captain, were moored offshore in Holehaven Creek from Holehaven Point towards Pitsea. They received gunpowder stored in caves in Benfleet Creek. On the Canvey side were boats named *Swift, Amy, Mineroa, Pilgrim, Diamond, Gem* and *Woodpark*. There were three others on the Corringham side.

Dynamite hulks are referred to by Coulson Kernahan (1858-1943) in *Captain Shannon*, 1897. After a description - "No one who has not visited Canvey would believe that so lonely and out of the world a spot could be discovered at a distance of 30 miles from London" - he goes on to tell of "the evil-looking dynamite hulks, which lie scowling on the water, like huge red coffins". Then there were 12 of them. Because Canvey was so out of the way he doubted if any more secure place could be found for them.

Sir Max Pemberton wrote a story round them; *Diamond Ship* (1907). Another writer, between the two, was Robert Buchanan who, before he died in 1901, wrote *Andromeda* (1900), partly based on Canvey. The writer drew attention to various centres of habitation that no one else had done. He spoke of four, rather contradicting those who had considered the Island as an entity. Judging by their names, they were mainly

Lobster Smack and Coastguards' lookout

based on extensive farms. Reference is also made to
the extensive bird life.

I like to think that the following extract from
Rivers of Great Britain (1897) is not quite so un-
complimentary as might appear. It also raises some
interesting points.

"A small boat soon shoots round the Lower
Hope and into the westerly channel that flows around
Canvey Island. At high tide the boat will travel easily
up to the sea-wall, which rears itself like a strong
fortification at the innermost edge of the saltings. The
wall is overgrown with sea-weed, and the very steps
by which one gains the Coastguard Station are slippery
with sea-grass. Inside the wall the stretch of the
island lies, as it were, in a great basin. Corn waves,
bright meadows shine in the summer, and marshy
streams creep slowly into the channels that cut the
weird place away from the mainland. A wild and for-
bidding place is Canvey Island. The strong sea-wall is
gruesome with its shaggy wreaths of trailing weed.
The inner side is well covered with coarse grass, and
from thence away to the northward a flat of some-
what repulsive aspect runs as far as Benfleet. The
island has a peculiar population. The coastguards'
hamlet lies close to the wall, and the men are
ordinary sailors; but in the villages of Canvey, Knights·
wick, Panhole, and Lovis, there is a scant population
of people who have their own ways, their own trad-
itions, and their own methods of regarding a stranger.
They are singularly hospitable, for free-handed sportsmen find the island a happy hunting-ground, and the
people expect and give kindness. The one little inn by
the Coastguard Station is, perhaps, the quaintest in all
Essex. Memories of smugglers, of desperate water
thieves, of old collier sailors seem to hang about its
low walls. No one need expect comfort there, but the
keeper purveys for all comers with a rude hospitality
which is amusing. On the Fobbing side of the Island
the ditches are very deep, and the sides soft and
treacherous. Once a bird is shot there it is very
difficult to recover it. All the dogs kept on the Island
have a singularly business-like air, but no one would
care to let a valuable dog follow his game down these

The Ford. Old Benfleet Station in background

steep, gluey, ramparts. To the east, however, the saltings stretch far towards Canvey Point; and it is not only safe, but absolutely pleasant to walk over them before the tide creeps through the rough herbage.

"Hardly a shore-bird known in the British Islands fails to visit Canvey. Looking through a telescope from Benfleet Station it is easy to pick out the flocks as they consort in their different communities, and squat among the mud, or pick their way carefully through the twining grass. At one time, on a frosty morning, it is possible to see dotterels, plovers, redshanks, gulls, and pipers, all busy on the eastern flats; while to the west the cunning curlews dodge on the slippery banks of the Fobbing ditches. The foreshore is perfectly free to strangers; although one proprietor in the island has ventured to dispute the fact. A private grant of the shore was made two hundred years ago, and below the sea-wall no visitor can be considered as a trespasser, while a boat may bring up anywhere in the channel. Canvey is not an inviting spot for camping out. On a gusty night, when the rushes moan and shiver, and the great river sounds hoarsely, it is hardly possible to look out into the darkness without feeling a sense of strangeness and even of fear. The island seems to have no salient points; the hill, topped by the house known as the Hall, rises a little, but it is more like a cloud than a solid mound. A shadowy figure from the coastguards' hut sometimes paces up and down, but even this gives none of the refreshment of human companionship. The writer once took refuge in the Channel at midnight during very bad weather. The boatmen did not care to land, and we sheltered ourselves as best we could from the storm. The island then showed in all its mystery through the drift of rain and the flying haze. It was an experience never to be forgotten; but no one is recommended to try it. It is better to seek the hospitable shelter of an inn, and put up with rough fare, or any fare, rather than remain in the open amid that abomination of desolation.

"The sea-wind comes with sharp stirring breath after we pass the long spit that shoots out from the weird island; the river is still yellow, but when the

Cox's Cafe and Dance Hall, Eastern Esplanade

breezes set the foam dancing the crests of the waves are of pure white."

On 29th November, 1897 (thenceafter known as 'Black Monday'), there was another flood. I well remember being told how the seawater penetrated to the centre of the Island. There, at Lakeside Corner, it remained for weeks. Remedial works then kept Canvey flood-free for more than half a century. The walls stood firm on 1st November, 1921, and again on 6th January, 1928, when there was flood damage along the coast. Canvey was still very rural then and I recall my parents took food supplies upstairs, in case there was a flood. It didn't disturb their slumbers and all was well in the morning. On 6th February, 1938, the barricades held, as they did in 1952, although the walls were damaged then. It was not until the gale-lashed night of 31st January/1st February, 1953, that the cruel sea tried again to take back to its own those proud acres that had for so long resisted its attacks. Once again, the Island counter-attacked and, with national help, threw the intruder back and restored some land by the damming of Small Gains and Tewkes Creeks.

The Way about Essex also published at the turn of the century, gives further evidence of its wild life. In the section on 'shooting information' it is recorded that "Sportsmen here must confine themselves to the sea wall and the saltings, but sailing or punting round the island may be indulged in without hindrance. There are always quantities of curlews and other shore birds round the island, and on the Thames shore many Brent geese may generally be found, as well as many other kinds of fowl". Sportsmen visiting Southend are advised that excursions may be made round the northern shore of Canvey and along the Chapman Sands for duck, teal, widgeon, and geese. Little can be done from the shore; a punt is 'absolutely necessary'. Yachtsmen were advised "A sail round Canvey may be managed if the draught be not too much".

The book also noted that portions of an ancient building were still visible at St Katherine's church.

The impact of modern civilisation was, however, on its way to Canvey Island and it came through the

Rev. Henry Hayes; John Harrison and William Wood, churchwardens

efforts of the Rev. Henry Hayes, who was educated at King's College, London, and who was a Past Provincial Grand Chaplain of Essex Freemasons. He came to Canvey at the age of 34 and served the Island 28 years before he died on 8th December, 1900, of cancer. He was appointed curate in charge in 1872; when Canvey became a separate civil and ecclesiastical parish he became Vicar.

Mr Hayes was instrumental in the rebuilding of the parish church, the building of the vicarage in 1873, and a church school in 1874. He became a Canvey Island Commissioner on 14th May, 1879, and later Vice-Chairman.

Queen Victoria's golden jubilee of 1887 was celebrated with a parish pump in 1889; financed by public subscription and a contribution from the Corporation of the City of London of 50 guineas, it was opened by the Chairman of the Port Sanitary Committee on 5th December, 1889. It was vested in a permanent committee of which the Rev. Hayes was an ex-officio member.

The 312 feet deep well was at the centre of the Island, at what is now the junction of Canvey/Long and Haven Roads. It had an unusual and possibly unique, thatched, high-point roof and was Dutch in character, designed by Clement Skilbeck. The metal plaque it bore inside was, after it had been demolished in the early 1930s as part of the road widening, inserted in the road. It was later put in Canvey Dutch Cottage Museum. Although weatherbeaten it is still legible. Inside the pump were wooden slatted seats and an inscription that read 'Whosoever drinketh of this water shall thirst again, but whosoever drinketh of the water that I shall give him shall never thirst.' Southend Waterworks Company borehole at Leigh Beck started pumping into supply in 1922.

The Vicar also spoke out strongly when he felt the need arose. A footnote to an 1893 burial entry said "I protested against the unsatisfactory nature of the inquest no medical evidence being taken as to actual cause of death."

Some idea of the still rural nature of the Island can be gathered from *The Sketch* ('Small Talk'; 13

The Stepping Stones, c.1905

September, 1893), which says, "How many, or perhaps I should say how few, of my readers, can tell me where is Canvey Island? I must confess that a few weeks ago I could not have answered my own question, being absolutely ignorant of its existence.

"The pleasures of Canvey Island were revealed to me by two lady artists whose work is well-known in several London papers, and who have a happy knack of finding out places that are 'far from the madding crowd' though within a few miles of the metropolis.

"Canvey Island, then, is close to the mouth of the Thames, on the Essex coast, and if one can enjoy a holiday minus smart folks and fashionable frocks, plus some five miles by two of marsh and pasture land, of sweet salt breezes, glorious sunsets, a con- stant procession of the shipping of the greatest commercial river in the world, and the bed and board of a comfortable farmhouse, then by all means make your arrangements for a holiday on Canvey island. By-the-way there are some 50 or so other houses, I should think, besides the one I have mentioned, on the island, and there is a church, a vicar, and a vicar's wife; the Island, too, is extremely respectable in the matter of age, and it is said, was written of in the long ago by Ptolemy, who called it 'Convennos'."

It was during Rev. Hayes' period of office that the Parish Council (established under the Parish Councils' Act of 1894) was first formed with 5 councillors, he being one of them. Mr Hayes was a far-seeing man. Having provided the basic necessities - education, both religious and secular, plus an adequate supply of water - he saw that what Canvey needed was easy access.

When he came to the Island one gingerly balanced over by stepping stones at low tide or came by ferry boat at other times. He wanted a bridge to link the Island with the mainland. About a month before he died Rochford Rural District Council (of which Canvey was then a part) in compliance with his wish, adjourned the matter till their next meeting when he could put it in detail. He never attended that meeting and it was not until 19th December, 1929, when the Ministry of Health held an enquiry at the

Colvin Bridge, 1931

Council school that there was more action. In March, 1930, the Ministry of Transport sanctioned its building. They contributed half the actual cost - equal to a contribution of £9,263. Consulting Engineer was H J Dean, B.E., M.Inst.C.E.: the contractor was A E Farr.

The first pile of the Colvin swing bridge was driven into the thick mud of Canvey-Benfleet creek (on the Canvey side) on 21st May, 1930. The inauguration was performed by Brigadier General R B Colvin, C.B., then Lord Lieutenant of Essex. Exactly a year later, on 21st May, 1931, Alderman John H Burrows, J.P., of Southend performed the opening ceremony. Schoolchildren lined the pavements as a stream of vehicles and organisations (with Canvey Chamber of Trade members in the lead) came over.

The bridge was opened for the last time on 26th November, 1968, and demolished in February, 1973, when replaced by a new one.

This was a long time in the future as the Rev. Hayes was buried in a plain English coffin with brass mounts at Highgate Cemetary by the Rev. A B Bennett. As the 10.27 a.m. train steamed out of Benfleet Station with his body, Canvey was about to be 'Hesterised'.

Of all those who have contributed to Canvey's development, Mr Frederick B Hester exercised powers that today are immortalised in property and title deeds all over the Island.

He planned to turn it into a seaside residential holiday resort with a European flavour. 'Little Holland' and using dykes as Venetian canals were two of the means. He started the development of Winter Gardens, a mono-rail was built, he sold property extensively, disposed of land through auctions, and had other plans, which, had he been able to fully implement them, would have transformed Canvey Island beyond recognition. He utilised the emerging science of publicity to its full and brought the name of Canvey Island to the attention of thousands of people.

In 1901, 1,004 plots of land were laid out for building in Southview Estate, part of Leigh Beck Farm. This was the start of a period of intensive holiday development on the Island lasting until 1905. By 1904

The horse-drawn mono-rail, c.1904

it was possible to see what Hester had achieved. A land auction at Whitsun that year brought in £600, its approach from Benfleet was marked by a large wooden tower, a mile of Winter Gardens had been built with glasshouses, 400 ft of the pier had been constructed and a horse-operated mono-rail was to be replaced with an electric railway.

By the summer of that year the electric tramway, with a power station, was under construction. On the ballasted permanent way over 4,000 creosoted sleepers had been unloaded and some laid. At a cost of £48,000 industrialists were to have handy light factories available. By August about 1,000 tons of ballast had been laid and 2½ miles of line provided. To carry passengers there were four 25 seater cars, enamelled red with a gold lining; to complete the effect there were window curtains. The vehicles bore the proud name 'Venice on Sea and Canvey' in gilt, for Mr Hester had ambitious plans to make the Island a modern Adriatic area with gondolas traversing the waterways (the dykes the Dutch had put in).

His plans were further enhanced by the arrival of 2,000 visitors in July. Land sales continued to bring in the cash to the tune of a thousand pounds.

During September and October the work was hurried on and overtime working, including Sundays, was authorised. A total of 200 tons of concrete had been laid and an engine was put on the rails. It brought truckloads of material from the barges discharging at the pier.

This was the summit; from now on it was to become the end of the line. Earlier the Scottish contractors had been compensated to the extent of £1,000 because the line had been delayed due to difficulty in the shipment of 30 ft. rails (gauge 3'6").

In October there was occasional delay in the delivery of materials. In November work stopped and notices went up on materials to say that they were the property of contractors.

On 7th April, 1905, at Chimney's Farm, near Winter Gardens, new electric tramway materials were sold by auction. The auctioneer had been instructed by an officer appointed by the County Court of Essex,

Canvey Pier, c.1902

held at Southend. Sold were 49 pitchpine standards, 23 ft long, 8 inches square at the base and 6 inches at the top, plus 1,000 of the sleepers.

Contractors had removed part of the tramway and the failure of the scheme was laid at the door of one person, who would not let the trams go over his property. A land development scheme (Central Park Estate) was in liquidation.

In 1906 more of the tramway was removed, but on 11th April that year, Canvey did get more permanent transport. A bus service ran from Leigh Beck to Benfleet in 45 minutes for a sixpenny fare - a charge that remained until the bridge was opened in 1931.

The pier survived for some years before being demolished. It was the only development of Mr Hester's that seems to be recorded on the Ordnance Survey. A length of 220 yards was shown on Sheet 73 (Chelmsford) of the O.S. (two miles to one inch) of 1907 (reduced from the one inch map of 1903-4).

Canvey, thus dragged into the 20th century by two people, continued to develop and attract residents, despite its lack of access.

It was in this period that the Baptist Church was to establish itself on the Island*. In 1900 non-conformists met in Leigh Beck Cafe, where they worshipped. In 1902 a former auction room was hired as the congregation had become larger and, in 1903, it was bought by a London merchant. It was rebuilt and became a hall - the Union Mission, afterwards called a Union Chapel. Then it was bought by a retired solicitor and pastor with strong Baptist leanings. A Sunday School was started in 1910. In 1923 the hall was practically rebuilt and two vestries were added in 1924. The church was taken over by the Baptist Union of Great Britain and Ireland and became the Baptist Church.

The church was going strongly on the Island and, in 1926, a second hall was built, in Winter Gardens, at a cost of £350, the ground having been given by a well-known Canvey benefactor, George Chambers. This became Winter Gardens Baptist

*The earliest known Essex register dates from 1775, Congregationalists 1707, Methodists, 1793.

St Anne

Mission. In 1929 an annexe was put on the front of the church.

A manse was erected in 1946 and in 1951 a youth hall was put up. This was to have a double purpose, for that year the main building was damaged by fire. The hall was undamaged and church services were held there until the main building had been repaired.

A new church was planned in 1965. On Saturday, 13th June, 1970, Arthur C Mason (life deacon) laid a foundation stone on behalf of members and congregation. On 5th September, 1970, the new building, erected at a cost of £13,950, was opened by the Rev. T W Shepherd, of Belle Vue Baptist Church, Southend, who carried out the dedication. An address was given by the Rev D M MacKenzie of Avenue Road Baptist Church, Southend.

The Church of England had found it necessary to expand too. It was in 1910 that St Anne's Church was built, of ferro-concrete. On 5th November, 1910, the church was opened for worship, the Bishop of Barking, Thomas Stevens, performing the ceremony. The bell, put there in 1911, commemorated the Coronation of George V. A church hall was opened in the grounds in November, 1931. In the 1953 flooding the church suffered and, on Thursday, 13th May, 1954, the Archdeacon of Southend (the Ven. W N Welch) conducted a rehallowing ceremony in the redecorated building.

On Saturday, 9th June, 1973, a stonelaying ceremony in connection with the new church took place, performed by the Venerable Peter Bridges, Archdeacon of Southend, and on 23rd November, 1974, the Bishop of Bradwell dedicated a new purpose-built church and hall at St Anne's to replace the demolished church and hall. The Bishop had been welcomed at the door by the Archdeacon of Southend, the Rev. Geoffrey J Wrayford (Vicar of Canvey) and the Rev. Keith Dickerson (assistant curate, who was leaving at the end of the year). It cost £30,000, with furnishings an extra £3,000. The bell from the former church was retained. Taken from the old building was a simple plaque, recording that Robert J H Monteith, licensed

Benfleet Station

lay reader, a private soldier of the Essex Regiment, died on 6th September, 1918, aged 26.

After the hiatus left by the bankruptcy in 1905 of Frederick Hester (who later received his discharge), the Island seemed to rest for a while, but 1911 proved to be an eventful year.

3rd March saw the formation of a Women's section of a Liberal & Labour Association (the main association, named South Benfleet and Canvey was active a year later). In the dock strike the Canvey policeman was transferred to Tilbury, where he remained; his place was taken by the Benfleet policeman who did duty for both districts.

The year was marked on 9th December by the new Benfleet Station being opened (the original had been burnt down on 3rd March, 1903, having been opened in 1855). Switched on were over 60 100 c.p. Cox's air gas lamps. Work had taken 18 months on the massive structure and piles had had to be driven between 34 and 37 feet deep to carry the structure round the booking hall. I remember the hall very well indeed, lit by flickering lamps and with a wooden seat running all the way round. All concrete work was re-inforced with old railway lines and all the walls were on 25 ft. piles, the covered portion of the platform was on 34 ft. piles. The brickwork was indeed picturesque, finished in roughcasting of the Elizabethan period. The platforms were 700 feet long. Work was completed by Christmas.

Towards the end of 1911, a Canvey Medical Association was founded, with officers and a general committee of 32 members, the object being to provide a resident medical officer for the Island with free or assisted treatment for the needy. A subscription list showed the names of over 100 people, a very good response for those times.

Prior to this Canvey shared Benfleet's doctor and I have been told of the days when he rode to the Island on horseback. Virtually all transport then was horse, including the Coroner who drove over in his pony and trap to hold court in the parlour of the then 'Red Cow' public house at The Village. A reporter, arriving to cover such an occasion, was late and had

Leigh Beck, c.1914

to race the Coroner across fields, while the officer drove sedately along the hedge-lined dusty road.

By the following year the Island's population had reached an all-time high of 543 (compared with 300 in 1901). Weather and its effects were still feared: a rain storm lashed the Island's fields in Saturday, 2nd March. Later in the year (21st November) the sea claimed another victim when a collusion occurred off the Chapman lighthouse. The coal-laden Hull schooner *William and Alice* foundered.

The Islanders were as determined as ever to keep the invader from their lands and the Ecclesiastical Commissioners, who then owned a quarter of the Island (collecting an annual rent of £750), paid out 25% of the annual seawall cost of £800. In those days £200 was certainly worth a lot more than it is now!

Canvey had not lost all trace of Mr Hester, for he was then acting as agent to look after land bought from the trustee in bankruptcy.

Some idea of the Island can be gained from a local estate agent who said that parts were like a jungle, with thistles, grass and hedges 'growing breast high, which would puzzle a Philadelphia lawyer to get through'.

Access was still via the ferry and creek-bed at low water. Repairs to the hard had to have Port of London Authority permission.

As August, 1914, blossomed it found an Island ready. Before the guns were stilled in 1918 the War god had reaped a harvest of 20 of the Island's population. It was not the first time Essex men had gone abroad for King and Country. At the Battle of Crecy and at Neville's Cross in 1346 200 county archers were in action.

As the Great War ended and those that were left returned to Canvey, they added to its population, which in 1921 stood at 1,795. The Island was much as they had left it and still without dry access. It would be well to take a closer look at the next decade, because it would be the last before Canvey gained what had long been wanted, and for which Mr Hayes had worked so long - a bridge.

The Island was still predominantly a residential

The Ford and Stepping Stones, c.1920

and agricultural area, but with a rising commuting population. People made their own bridges across the many dykes draining the Island. An enterprising builder was advertising telegraph poles, 26 ft and 28 ft long as new, and describing them as suitable for bridges. The prices were £2 and £2.10s. each.

For bungalows galvanised corrugated iron, 6 ft x 7 ft, was available. It was 'splendid, stout, as new' at 11d [4½p] a foot run.

The Rev. Edwin Green became Vicar in 1919. In 1921 he lost his licensed lay reader, but was joined for a temporary period by one who had done good work as a Captain in the Church Army and had served in France.

It was not only the church that had ex-service members. A jobbing gardener 'passed by Board of Agri-culture - speciality pruning' proudly described himself as an ex-sergeant.

Work was going on with the restoration of the Parish Church. The foundation had been rebuilt, the sanctuary floor relaid and, by March, the interior was being repaired. Future plans included painting the church outside and repairing 'thoroughly' the roof.

Premises (later burnt down) became available for hire for 'concerts, public meetings, whist drives, beanfeasts, dances, school treats, etc.'. The energetic Rev. Green had been joined by a temporary helper, the Rev. H A Powell, and he was to hold a series of spec-ial services in the building known as The Rendezvous, as would St Anne's Sunday School.

Canvey was attracting more distinguished visitors too. The Bishop of Barking paid his first visit on Sun-day, 24th July, 1921, when he preached at the Parish Church on behalf of the Church Missionary Society.

The Church of England Day School buildings were in bad repair in the summer of 1921. Remedial work would cost from £60 to £100. The school man-agers had promises of £45 'contingent upon the whole work being taken in hand' and there was a debt of £26 for repairs already done.

In the past a voluntary rate had kept it going, but now few were able to respond to the managers' request. Instead they asked for a voluntary rate of

Mr G Machin and the schoolchildren, 1912

threepence in the pound or for donations. In October
the Vicar sounded a warning note in his parish
magazine that "If Church people do not feel inclined
to support their own schools, they must not feel
aggrieved if the school is unable to be kept up and
has to make way for a Council school". This, of
course, was what would happen eventually, despite the
efforts of all concerned.

In December, 1921, Mr & Mrs G Machin retired
from the school; Mrs Robertson, who had worked as a
nurse in Egypt in the war, came as Head Teacher.

Then came a threat to the Parish Church. The
authorities suggested that it would be better to shut it
up and build at the other end of the Island. But the
Vicar said "It would be a pity to close it just now
because it is not largely attended" and urged better
support. A combined vestry and annual parochial
church meeting on 19th April, 1922, unanimously said
"In the opinion of this meeting it is inexpedient to
transfer the Parish Church to a new site at the other
end of the Island for two strong reasons: 1) The historical continuity would be broken 2) New develop-
ments, such as making of sea wharves or docks may
occur within a short time, rendering it necessary that
St Katherine's should be a large and important
church."

If church attendances were dropping, the school
roll was not and, with an accommodation for 69, there
were, on 20th June, 1922, 97 present out of 104.

Canvey's connections with the sea were tragic-
ally emphasised on 27th May, 1922, when a seaman of
a Spanish naval ship was buried. He was 21 and had
been drowned off Hole Haven. He was laid to rest in
St Katherine's churchyard by the Roman Catholic
priest, Father Gilbert. The crew of the vessel and a
party from the Coastguard Station attended.

Tragedy struck again in March, 1924, when S.S.
Matatua and S.S. *American Merchant* (on its maiden
voyage to Tilbury) were in collision off Hole Haven. A
number of men were killed outright.

Seedtime and harvest time were still proceeding
with their age-old rhythm and harvest thanksgiving
services were observed at the two Island churches with

"Welcome Hut" & Sea Wall, Canvey on Sea

Welcome Hut at south of Furtherwick Road, c.1925

corn, flowers fruit, vegetables and bread.

In 1923 it was suggested that a new church and vicarage should be built at Leigh Beck, but this was again resisted.

In that year Canvey Island Public Interests' and Ratepayers' Association built a beach shelter. In 1924 a room to hold 60 children was built near the school and that was to come in very handy later.

Easter, 1924, brough record holiday crowds, encouraged by the fine weather. In the August Bank Holiday of 1924 15,000 visitors crossed by rowing boat to the Island. Demands were made for a bridge - fruitlessly, of course.

But times were hard. Canvey Public Interests and Ratepayers' Association discussed the price of bread: it had gone up in 8 days by three farthings for a two-pound loaf. Members were told that flour, 38 shillings in June, had risen to 51 shillings and they were advised to eat cake!

It was in that year that the school provided through the efforts of Mr Hayes had to close, due to its size, lack of equipment and distance from the centre of population. In October, 1924, William Dring Read, B.Sc., Assistant Master at Charles Street School, Birmingham, was appointed as Headmaster of the new Council School (which later became a Secondary School) and, during the years to follow, he was to make his mark in the developing community, not only as a scholastic leader and churchman, but also as a Councillor (from 1929 to 1935, being Vice-Chairman 1930/1). The present, re-built school is named after him. He was born at Norwich in 1885 and died on 15th June, 1952, after 21 years Headmastership, during which time the population had more than trebled; he had retired in 1945. He had been a member of Canvey Food Control Committee and a member of South East Essex Divisional Executive, Essex Education Committee. A keen churchman, he had been Vicar's Warden for 18 years, a licensed reader for 25 years and a member of the Church Council.

At his funeral service the Rev. A J Mortimer described him as a 'great schoolmaster and a great Churchman'. He said, "We bury this morning one of

St Katherine

the great schoolmasters of Canvey."

On 1st May, 1922, a parish meeting to consider a school site was held. Of two sites offered by George Chambers (Parish Council Chairman) Little Gypps North was selected. On Tuesday, 7th October, 1924, the school was opened to the singing of the school song, 'Play the game'. The next day school work started. The Rev. Green records "The number of new scholars entered was so large that the managers at once held an emergency meeting and requested the Education Committee to move the temporary hut from the village school. The Committee met next day and consented to this necessary step being taken. No child will be refused admission whilst the school is being enlarged."

The building was to serve the Island well, being bombed in the 1939 War and serving as a Rest Centre in the 1953 flood, before being replaced. But the village schoolroom (where the old Parish Council had met) was not forgotten and was used as a social centre. It became the Village Hall in 1925. It was gutted by fire on 14/15th April, 1954 .

A decisive step had been taken to carve out a new Canvey. No longer was the education of its children to be carried out at the old Village School.

Some other essential services were still basic, only 129 properties being connected to the water main. Next would be an alteration in local government, but the work of the Parish Council would not go unrecorded. A special service was held on 3rd May, 1925, at the Parish Church to inaugurate its new year of office; less than a year later, on 7th April, 1926, the new Urban District Council held its first meeting.

It was in May, 1925, that two notable deaths were observed. The burial took place of Mrs Hayes, thus severing the final link with a man who had served Canvey faithfully and well. On Empire Day, the congregation stood in silent tribute for the death of the Earl of Ypres.

Meanwhile the vestry at the Parish Church was being rebuilt and a vestry was planned for St Anne's, the little church, then an island within an island, for its land was almost encircled by a broad dyke.

The Rev. A W Cotton had been appointed Chap-

The Chapel
Convent of the Good Shepherd
Canvey Island, Essex.

Convent of the Good Shepherd

lain to the Convent Chapel of the Community of the Good Shepherd, the chapel being consecrated by the Bishop of Chelmsford in 1924. The Convent advertised in the parish magazine - "The Sisters will be glad of orders for work - frocks, coats, hats, fancy bags, etc. Also for orders for toffee, coconut ice and other sweets. Prices on application."

Although the Chapel, in Oyster Fleet, was primarily for private worship by the Sisters, by courtesy of the Mother Superior and by Mr Green's permission, it was open to the public for certain specified services.

In 1925 the Vicar welcomed the Rev. W Phillips as pastor of the Baptist Church.

In December, 1925, it was decided by the Church Council to enlarge St Anne's by a 30 ft x 10 ft building on the north side. This would serve as a vestry and a Sunday-School classroom. It would also provide accommodation for some of the large attendances at festivals and in the summer. Cost of enlargement and repairs was estimated at about £130.

In 1926 the number of inhabited houses was 1,716 and there was overcrowding at the Council School, described in His Majesty's Inspector's report as 'very serious'. There were 360 children attending: recognised seating accommodation, including the temporary wooden building, was 250. There were five rooms with numbers in each of them of 73, 71, 71, 66 and 75. The Headmaster, with an assistant teacher, took the top class. The majority of pupils were aged 5 to 13.

During that year St Anne's had an anonymous donation of an oak porch, while St Katherine's churchyard was enlarged. The first Civic Service was held on 16th May, when the Bishop of Chelmsford was the preacher. A memorial to the fallen in the Great War in the form of a wall with a tablet containing the names and with a public fountain in the foreground was unveiled on land given by Mr Chambers in Long Road.

But even as the Island hallowed its war dead the casulties were still being reported. In June, 1926, Mr Green noted the death of a man of 43 who 'fought

The Elms Lending Library, Small Gains Corner

Bond's Stores, Maurice Road

London Road, c.1925. Steven's Bakery on left

for Canvey in the war. He passed through much suffering then...'

And it was not only the war survivors who were dying. The following issue of the Parish Magazine tells the death of another Island pioneer, John Harrison, of Waterside Farm. Mr Harrison had been prominent as a churchwarden, member of the Parish Council, manager of the school and a Wall Commissioner.

Frederick J Leach, who succeeded Mr Harrison at the same farm (now in Council ownership and turned into a Sports Centre), in his turn became Chair man of the Wall Commission and a member and Chairman of Canvey Urban Council.

On Saturday, 1st August, Canvey-on-Sea Horti-cultural Society staged a flower, fruit and vegetable exhibition and sports on St Anne's Cricket Field, near Lufferies Farm. Star opener was the M.P. for the area, W H Looker. I am indebted to Aubrey Stevens for a copy of the schedule of an occasion described as 'very enjoyable'. The Rev. Green was treasurer and Vice-President. Among the many classes was one for children under 14 for bunches of locally-gathered wild flowers. The advertisements make interesting reading: of the firms three are still thriving - The Canvey Supply Co., Ltd., Tower Stores [now Tower Radio, Ltd.], and the newly-opened 'Haystack', whose prop-rietor and licensee, H J Dellaway (who was to become a Canvey Councillor) announced that he was late of the Strand, Little, Kingsway, and Garrick Theatres, London.

The Island's topography was a little uncertain. What is now the High Street was divided into three sections - London Road, High Road and Gains Road. However, Great Keats Road, at the eastern end of the community, had disappeared.

It was a record-breaking August Bank Holiday for the area, despite thunderstorms. From the heated streets of London tens of thousands poured down (mostly by train) to the Essex sea fronts. More than 50,000 of them came to Canvey, lining up six deep, up to an hour, to get across the ferry by one of four rowing boats.

By November, 1926, Mr Green was able to

A May Queen is crowned

14 Star Tea Gardens, Eastern Esplanade, c.1938

Suter's Stores, Gains Road, c.1920

report the enlargement of St Anne's was progressing as £103 of the required £120 had been collected. However he wrote, "Could we not go further and line the church with proclite, instead of the present canvas and also repaint the woodwork and generally put the structure in good repair?"

There was a shock for his parishioners. In the December magazine, under the dateline 20th November, the Vicar sadly announced, "I regret to say that I am under doctor's orders to lessen my work. I have, therefore, placed my resignation in the hands of the Bishop of Chelmsford, believing that, in the best interests of our large and continually increasing population, I am doing right in making way for a younger and more vigorous man." His resignation was dated to take effect in May, 1927.

It was typical of Mr Green that four days after penning this notice he should preside at a meeting in Canvey Hall to form a Canvey Troop of Baden-Powell Boy Scouts. The Scoutmaster was a well-known boy's author, Geoffrey Prout.

And soon, with the departure of Mr Green, another chapter in Canvey's development closed. Mr Green had had his triumphs with the improvements to his churches, the forming of organisations and the widening of horizons. Perhaps it was sad that the link between school and church had, to some extent, been broken by the establishment of a Council School. It did mean, though, that Canvey's ever-increasing younger population would continue to receive an even better education and that provision could be made to give evening tuition for those who felt they had a need of it.

Commercially too the Island was developing, for while the issue of the Parish Magazine for January, 1921, had 21 advertisments, that of December, 1926, held 31.

They had been years of progress to which the Rev. Reginald Chute (1927-8) and the Rev. Edward Dobree (1928-36) were to see further moves.

With the building - at long last - of a bridge to connect the Island with the mainland and the lowering, widening and improving of the old High

A typical Canvey bungalow, c.1910. Built by K Sheppard, Gains Road. "Bungalows from £125"

Road, Canvey was to develop even more during the years that lay before World War II. Oil storage tanks were also built during the 30s.

That period saw the number of bungalows ever increase - at Canvey Village, in Long Road (Southwick Estate, etc.), off Furtherwick Road (Labworth, Ash, Elm Roads, Marine Avenue, etc.). There was a new Dutch Village off Canvey Road. Some idea of current prices can be gleaned from the following details. In 1932-3 (population 3,530) Creeksea Tea House in the High Street served lunches at 1s.6d. (7½p.) and dinner for 3/- (15p). In 1933 brick-built bungalows at Canvey Village were offered at £385.

Another builder offered bungalows 'for an agreed deposit, not exceeding £50 and 10s. (50p.) weekly'.

An estate agent offered plot prices: Furtherwick Park (concrete road, water and light) £12; Kloster Park (only 12 left) £10; Village Green (water and light) £10; Canvey Park III £12; Oysterfleet £8.10s; Winter Gardens £7; Sixty Acres £6.10s. The Island was sewered in 1934-6 and ambulance and fire services were provided. In 1936 the population was 3,532 (the Church roll was 213) and there was a cinema. In 1937 ("The new cigarette 10 for 6d, 20 for 1s.") property was freely advertised to let - "bungalows... all newly decorated and in first class condition with every modern convenience; gas, company's water, electric light, concrete roads"; lounge, living room, kitchenette, two bedrooms 16s. a week; another, hall, lounge, living room, tiled kitchenette, two bedrooms, and bathroom £1 a week. Rentals included all rates and taxes, wall rate and water rate. In that year land was advertised for sale - "four or eight plots, 10 ft. x 90 ft. Made-up road, electric, main water, gas. Close to bus stop - Bargain, £20 a plot."

Further provision for the Island's spiritual needs was made. There had been for many years a strong Roman Catholic community. When, in 1912, a priest took over the Leigh Mission, it included Canvey. In those days going to Mass could take a whole morning. A walk to the ferry, a trip over (or a walk across the stepping stones) and then a train from Benfleet, plus

Our Lady and the English Martyrs

the whole expedition in reverse when returning.

Arrangements were made to hold Mass at the home of Mr Levi (a Jew) and his wife (a Roman Catholic). Eventually, Mr Levi became a Catholic and his two sons Jesuits. They built a wooden hut for Father (later Canon) Francis W Gilbert (1917-52), Parish Priest of Our Lady of Lourdes, Leigh, in their garden and he said his weekly Mass on the dressing table. Later Mass was said in other Island homes, including that of Dr William M Corbett.

In September, 1930, Islanders wrote to the Bishop asking for a local church. A site was generously given in Long Road by A M Clark. E E Lawrence designed an outstanding building, steel framed, with brick walls and a roof of green, glazed tiles. It seated 400.

On 12th March, 1937, Father Gilbert blessed the ground, sprinkled it with holy water and cut the first sod. The building was opened on Whit Monday, 1938. It was serviced from Leigh until Father John Watson took over in 1947.

In his trust deed, Father Gilbert left £1,000 for the erection of a church and presbytery at Canvey. The name of the church - Our Lady of Canvey and the English Martyrs - is derived from a beacon called Our Lady of Canvey. Father Gilbert, who had known the Island back in the 80s, had originally decided to dedicate it to St John Fisher and St Thomas More: instead he decided on the local link.

Light amusement was not neglected. Canvey Casino had been opened on the seafront in 1933.

A 105-page booklet of caravan and camp sites issued in March, 1937, listed a private enterprise site on the seafront opposite the Council's car park.

By the summer of 1938 there were 4,010 buildings with a rateable value of £40,315. In 1939 2,723 were able to enjoy main water. Little did they think, as they came to Canvey in those peaceful days, that a few years later they would be more than grateful for them. Many, bombed out of London by the German air-raids, were only too thankful that they had an alternative roof over their heads on the Island.

As the decade drew to its close the menacing

Casino and Labworth Cafe, 1933

signs of war were apparent. A Territorial Army battery was formed. Air Raid Precautions (the ubiquitous A R P of the 40s) was organised. A German aircraft took pictures of the Estuary, but fled before it could be intercepted. As the summer ended, so up went the blackout curtains as Britain went to war.

The Island Territorials manned their coastal guns. In 1940 the Battle of Britain was fought out overhead: one of the first German air-raids on England was in May, 1940, against the oil storage tanks near the 'Lobster Smack'.

An island that had last known invasion by the Dutch, now found itself right in the front line. Home Guards stood ready to defend it, the bridge had been mined so that if the enemy had managed to get a foothold they would not be able to cross the Creek with armour. The Benfleet Downs had been utilised to make slit-trenches from which the invaders' infantry would have faced a curtain of small-arms fire, had they attempted to force the Creek itself.

Canvey, now a defence area in which movement was restricted, prepared itself for a long war. It proved to be a struggle that once again took its toll of Island youth - their names are enshrined locally.

Canvey was to know bombs of every description and it was to have rockets land on its clay soil. Its firemen were to go to the aid of stricken towns and villages, leaving their main station and two sub-stations to do so.

Anti-aircraft guns were embrasured on the Island and nightly they took a toll of the Luftwaffe as they went up-river to attack London. With their aid a massive force of enemy aircraft in a daylight raid were forced to divert.

The Island's police force had been augmented by specials and, while there was little crime, there was plenty to do in enforcing war-time restrictions.

When the war ended Canvey could truly say that it had played its part in the conflict in every respect.

Now came the task of rebuilding the district. There were many problems, chief among them the Island's population which had increased substantially over the war years. Many of the residents, bombed

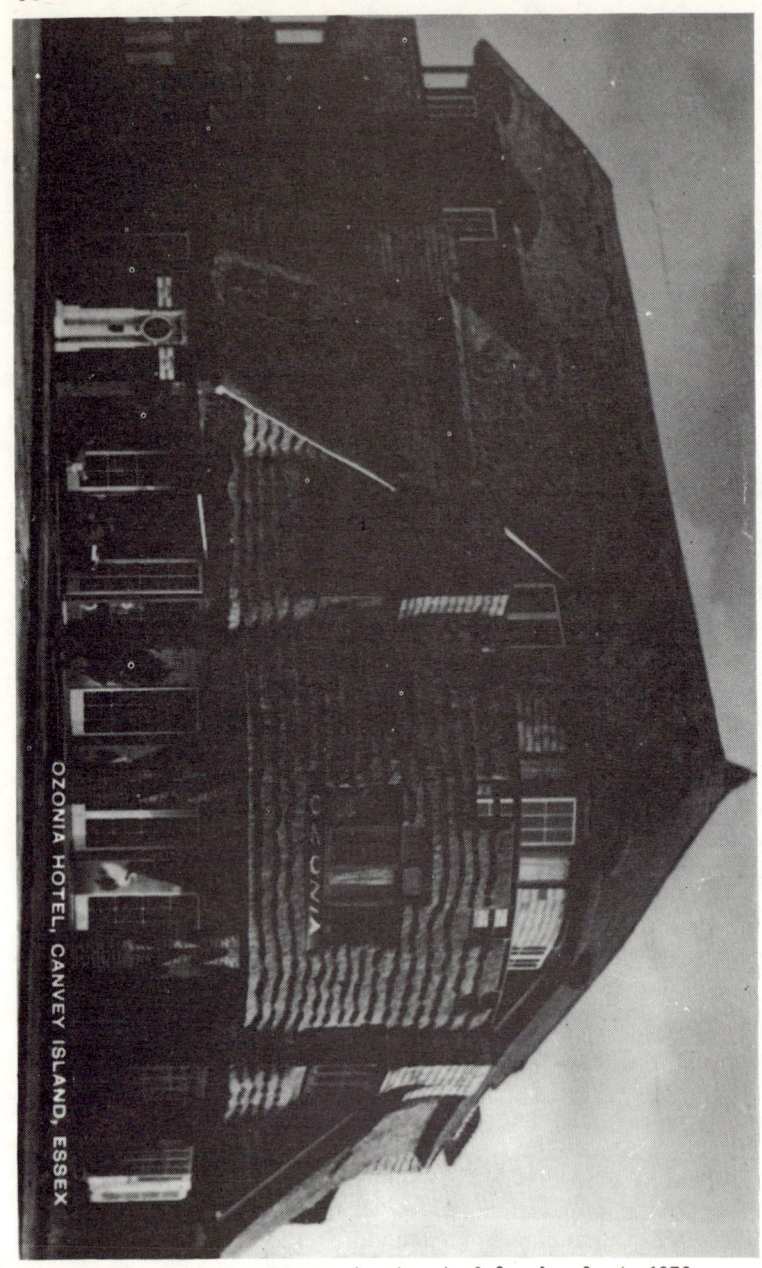

Ozonia Hotel, at the seafront end of Seaview Road, 1939

out, had come to their second homes at Canvey and had decided that they would continue to live in them. The population was now 10,030, but now the restrictions still in force would keep the rate of progress down.

Industry was, of course, of paramount importance. It had first started in 1936 and after the war it continued. On 19th April, 1948, Rex Parton, then Assistant Director, Board of Trade; G Hudson, Chairman of the Local Industrial Group, Board of Trade; leading officials and prominent Islanders inspected local factories. It was noted, by 1960, "Industrial development is now being centred on two excellent sites, admirably positioned, and Canvey Island Urban District Council gives every assistance to industrialists." Subsequently there were inquiries both at Canvey and at Benfleet into the building of oil refineries on the Island.

Canvey Council started to build council houses in 1947, as post-war restrictions meant very little private building on the Island. However, its popularity as a seaside resort continued to flourish. For the first time since 1939 people were able to get away for a break and they flocked down to the Island in their thousands.

It was already apparent that the Island's access left much to be desired. The ferry boats and the stepping stones had given way to the bridge in 1931, but with the level-crossing gates often in use and the bridge then closed to road traffic, there were often long queues of vehicles on a summer's night stretching tail-light to front bumper right across the Island. A high-level bridge was once again proposed and urged repeatedly, but to little avail. Money was short, there were (to other eyes) more important projects to be carried out and Canvey, to its regret, could get very little satisfaction.

By November, 1950, it was possible to draw up a balance sheet of roads and other services:

Highways could be divided into three categories: County Roads 5.87 miles (no post-war construction); District roads 8.31 miles (including 1.36 post-war); Private roads 8.47 miles (including 0.39 miles post-war): a total of 22.65 miles (1.75 post-war). Sewers

The Chapman Lighthouse

17.49 miles (4.84 being post-war). Water mains 39.7 miles (including 4.74 laid post-war). Gas mains 50 miles (with 1.1 miles post-1945). Electricity mains 37 miles.

In November, 1951, it was announced that work had started on a scheme to supply 17 roads with main water. This meant that an extra 250 properties would get, and over 93% of the Island would then have, the supply. Cost was over £2,000 for laying 3,777 yards of water mains.

The Second World War was still fresh in people's minds and in January, 1951, members of Canvey British Legion started building their own hall. A corner stone was laid by the President, George Curnick, on 19th June, 1951. Canvey played its part in the Festival of Britain when over 30 local organisations took part in activities from May to September.

These too were the years of the Korean War and, once again, Island lives were lost in a national conflict. Two Islanders were captured in the Glorious Gloucesters' last desperate stand at the Imjin River.

Canvey was to appear on the television screen for the first time. As has earlier been noted, the Chapman lighthouse was erected in the Thames Estuary in 1850 and equipped with lights in 1851: to celebrate its centenary the Island Yacht Club, in conjunction with the Canoe Club, made a presentation to the keepers on 23rd June. Yachts and canoes sailed out from Small Gains Creek and Hole Haven. The lighthouse was boarded and the keepers presented with a cake decorated with a model of the lighthouse, a suitable plaque, the arms of Trinity House, the Island Yacht and Canoe Club flags and the Festival of Britain badge. It was carved in mahogany by E Reddish and received by Principal Keeper Arthur E Ritter and Keeper Robert H Humphreys.

In August, the Regent Oil Company was granted a licence in the sum of £500,000 to develop a site of more than 30 acres at Canvey as an oil storage installation and depot. The main feature was a two-headed jetty running out 800 feet into the river. It was the Island's biggest industrial development.

Although industry was coming to the Island it

Haystack Corner, Canvey.

Haystack Corner

did not deter the holiday-makers and, during the August Bank Holiday, Thorney Bay Holiday Camp reported 'more than 7,000' visited there; this gave yet further impetus to the need for a better form of access. The needs of residents and visitors to enjoy the seafront were not neglected and beach improvement schemes were announced.

In December it was decided that a replacement Secondary School was to be built in Furtherwick Road to accommodate 600 children from 11 to 16. Canvey's rateable value was then £49,600.

It was in 1952 that a local inquiry was held into Canvey's case for its own seat on Essex County Council (hitherto shared with Benfleet). It was conducted by Roger Blenkiron Willis on 10th January at Benfleet Council Chambers and on 19th February it was announced that Canvey had won its case. The single seat was subsequently increased to two.

In that February a further 167 street lamps were planned to brighten the post-war darkness.

Two Canvey sportsmen who took part in the Helsinki Olympics in 1952 were Roland and Francis Prout, who equalled the time for the 1948 Olympics in the 100 metre canoe race. Later they became more renowned for the development of the catamaran (a twin-hulled sailing boat). The Prouts had a distinguished canoeing career: in July, 1951, they were part of the K.4 team that won the first National Champion ship event to come to Canvey. In the same season they were unbeaten in all K.2 National Championships. They set up British records for each of the 500, 1,000 and 10,000 metre distances. In 1951 they held 9 national championship plaques.

In August, 1952, a flood fund was started to help the stricken Devon town of Lynmouth that had been devasted by floods. The appeal was made by Councillor Leach, who was still to be Chairman of Canvey Council when the district suffered its own flood a few months later. In the first week over £140 was donated and by the time it closed on 20th September the fund had reached £215.2s.4d.

In September the Council split the Island into 5 wards with the number of Councillors increased to 15.

Furtherwick Corner, c.1930

By now the rateable value had crept up to £50,175. Since 1945 something over £1½M capital had been invested in the district. The summer population was estimated at 100,000. Indeed, a far cry from the days when Canvey first set out to become a seaside resort. There was further evidence of Canvey's startling growth in the 1951 Annual Report of the Medical Officer of Health; between the census of 1931 (3,530) and that of 1951 (11,255), Canvey's population had grown by 218%, the highest increase for Essex in that period. The total number of inhabited houses was 4,302.

The departure of the Rev. A J Mortimer was announced. He had come to Canvey on 10th March, 1945, and had been on the Island longer than any Vicar since Mr Green. He had performed nearly 1,000 baptisms.

So the year came to an end with the feeling that it hadn't been too bad a time. True, some restrictions, painful legacies of the war, were still in force, but the Minister of Works had issued a licence for the erection of three extra shops, plans were well ahead for the opening soon of a memorial hall to the Island's war dead, the date of next year's local Council elections had been advertised (9th May). Canvey organisations - and by now there were a great many of them - were asked by the Council to appoint 'in writing, a representative to serve on the Coronation Committee of the Council', the next meeting being held at the Council Offices on 12th January, 1953. And there was more cheering news on the municipal front - rateable value was now £53,426.

Islanders could be forgiven a glow of complacency as they sat down to hear the Queen's Christmas message. There was no sign that, as the first month of the New Year ended, Canvey Island would go through a traumatic experience needing all the courage of its residents to withstand and bringing tragedy unparalleled even by the years of war.

The Saturday of 31st January, 1953, was a squally one, with a growing force of wind, raving over the open fields with tremendous strength. It was a great occasion for the Island for, in the evening, the

The Floods, Canvey Island, 1953.

Craven Avenue, 1953

War Memorial Hall, built to honour the Island's slain of World War II, was to be opened by Captain Dennis Brown, J.P., a Deputy Lieutenant of Essex. Inside the building was a bronze plaque, listing the names of the 57 Islanders who had died.

As the large number gathered for the occasion they were not to know that this figure would be topped in less than 24 hours, when 58 would die in the floods. As the audience fought its way home against the increasing gale, they thought, pleasurably, of a week of events to follow to celebrate years of endeavour to raise funds to build the hall, which would make a pleasing milestone for the event.

It was shortly after 2 a.m. that the seawalls at the eastern end of the Island started to give way and the tide poured in. As a desperate measure to rouse residents to the peril Sub-Officer Frank Griffith, head of the Island's retained fire brigade, sounded the fire siren and fired maroons.

Those who were woken from sleep did what they could in the storm-tossed darkness to the screams of the trapped and the dying. Boats were launched, people were taken from flood-drenched homes, some to a temporary rest centre set up in the William Read School and others to the mainland, by a fleet of ambulances. The drivers found the remains of the High Road, which had been by-passed by the new road before the war, of great value. Where the latter was flooded, the old 'Danish Causeway' enabled them to get through.

Meanwhile Reginald Herbert Stevens, Canvey Urban Council's Engineer & Surveyor, took command of the situation and, as dawn broke over a shattered Island, he made the most momentous decision that has ever had to be taken in peacetime in this country - to evacuate the whole of the Island. Mainland vehicles came over and as many of the Island's 10,000 inhabitants as were willing to leave were taken to schools at Benfleet and other hurriedly set-up rescue centres.

It is not the British way to wave one's arms and generally make a spectacle of ones-self over such an incident and Mr Stevens once described the occasion in a clipped, military, no-nonsense sort of

Larup Avenue area, 1953

way. He said, "With all services knocked out the answer was to get the people to the mainland. At first they were reluctant to go. About 3,000 left by mid-day but, as more and more houses were flooded by the second tide, they realised the position and started to go in larger numbers."

In all, Mr Stevens organised the evacuation of 8,000 people. However, others still clung to their homes, determined not to leave until they were forced. As they did so, a vast army of workers poured on to the Island to reinstate its battered defences. Servicemen volunteers came in the biting winter weather to hurredly fill in the gaping wounds in the Island's seawall. Sandbags were mainly used to plug the gaps and by the Wednesday it was reported that the defences were once again watertight, by which time 36 bodies had been recovered.

Words were valueless at a time like this and names invidious in paying tribute to those who toiled so ceaselessly, careless of their own safety, to rescue, evacuate and comfort. Council staff, Councillors, firemen, ambulance staff, the Armed Services, religious organisations, and countless other voluntary bodies worked without remit to achieve what they did.

There was national recognition of the parlous state that Canvey was then in and Sir Winston Churchill, the Prime Minister, assured a crowded House of Commons on the Monday that the disaster would be treated on a national basis. Sir Winston said, "The disaster which has fallen on the inhabitants of Canvey Island seems to have been a most grievous one."

The Lord Mayor of London opened a distress fund. The following day (Tuesday) the Queen Mother and Princess Margaret saw Islanders when they visited a rest centre at a Benfleet school.

Then came the days, weeks, months, years of rebuilding. The walls continued to hold against the spring tides. The first factory re-opened. Then the first of the money to help came in: of £10,000 from the National Flood and Tempest Relief Fund to Essex, £2,500 went to Canvey and a local committee was appointed to deal with its allocation.

By 20th February the Eastern Electricity Board

Larup Avenue, 1953

were able to report that about 1,500 consumers (out of 3,400) were again being supplied. The Board's show-rooms were giving a seven-day service.

More figures emerged. The 'Red Cow' public house at Canvey Village had had 500,000 sandbags filled in its forecourt: the inn had been the head-quarters of the combined forces' work, named 'Operation King Canute'. As a lasting memorial – and with the brewers' agreement – the hostelry was renamed 'The King Canute' and its signboard commemorates the disaster.

Later in the month the House of Commons debated the flood and it was then that Bernard Braine*, Conservative Member for the district, spoke the epic words that have been more than fulfilled in the passing years. Mr Braine, who had laboured mightily in the intervening weeks, told a hushed House, "Make no mistake; Canvey Island will rise again."

Nearly twenty years later I wrote that, in 1953 he 'laboured without stint to better the conditions and restore the area. His voice was never silent locally or in the Houses of Parliament and he can truly claim to be one of the architects of the new, improved, safer Canvey which emerged from that period." It says much for the man that he had realised the Island's creed and had not hesitated to say it before the greatest in the land.

Before Mr Braine spoke there had been some defeatist talk – not, I hasten to add, on Canvey – when it had been suggested that the Island should be permanently evacuated or, slightly less seriously, that parts should be 'thrown to sea' and not permanently reclaimed again. After Mr Braine had spoken, no more nonsense like that was heard, although it had been a definite threat at one time.

On 4th March, the Lord Mayor of London, Sir Rupert de la Bere, toured the flood-stricken land and handed over a cheque for £20,000 from his fund to Council Chairman, Fred J Leach, and Council Clerk, Reg Whitley.

The month saw a degree of normality returning with the first wedding on the Island and Island teams

* Knighted in the 1972 New Year's Honours List.

Jones's Stores, Long Road, 1953

again playing soccer after a four-week lay-off.

Then came a new threat to Canvey. Sir Alan Herbert suggested in the *Essex Chronicle* that Canvey should be sacrificed to save London in times of flooding. Here I, personally, had to intervene and the newspaper subsequently published a reply from me (under the heading 'McCave of Canvey sends a challenge and tells Sir Alan Herbert he's wrong').

I refuted his defeatist attitude and suggested that the remedy was a separate Government Ministry to organise, co-ordinate and deal with our flood defences. I challenged him to 'come down to Canvey and to a mass meeting of our inhabitants' give those views. I ended 'No, Sir Alan, Canvey honours those who died in the floods. A living Canvey Island will be a permanent memorial to them.'

Sir Alan did not accept my challenge and nothing more was heard about his views. However, later in March a Coastal Flooding Committee was set up, known as the Waverley Committee after its Chairman, Viscount Waverley, who visited Canvey.

As Island schools re-opened the extent of their damage was reported. At Long Road Primary, during the flood aftermath a canteen built to serve 375 meals, but actually producing 900 a day, open from morning till late at night, with teachers and canteen staff working together.

Now, occasionally, were coming the valour awards. 2nd Canvey Troop Scoutmaster Arthur Bishop, J.P., got the Scout Medal for Meritorious Conduct for his flood rescue work; scouts, who had played a valiant part in the rescues were still helping to clean up, between 300 and 400 Scouts and Guides assisting.

Those who died in the flood were sharply recalled when a mass memorial service took place. As a result of the flood (against which it was not insured) Canvey War Memorial Hall - which had that inauspicious opening, after which it became a meals' centre for workers, was damaged to the tune of £340 and if plaster work was replaced this would cost a further £150. There was also £375 outstanding for the original building of the hall.

Then came the awaited announcement. The

Newlands

Off High Street

Islanders would hear plans for the new sea defences at a meeting on 30th April - at the War Memorial Hall.

Those present at the best attended meeting in the Island's history were told of a £500,000 plan to make the Island's walls the safest they had ever been by raising them between two and three feet. Steel sheet piling would be used and two creeks (Tewkes and Small Gains) dammed.

Some idea of the magnitude of the task facing those responsible for putting the Island's defences beyond peradventure can be gauged when it is considered that of 839 breaches along 310 miles of seawall controlled by the Essex River Board, 51 took place in Canvey's 15 miles (which were reduced by $2\frac{1}{2}$ miles by the creek damming).

By the following May five miles of the wall fronting the River Thames and along the badly breached wall around Sunken Marsh, interlocking steel piles had been driven into the seaward side of the wall. On the upper part of the clay barricades concrete block facing had been laid, jointed in bitumen. The piling had been reinforced with thousands of cubic yards of clay along about a mile of the wall. The two clay dams had also been faced with concrete blocks and stone. They held about 50,000 cubic yards of clay.

Statistics are commonly regarded as boring, except to the specialists, but the figures for this particular operation were of vital importance to the whole of the Island's population, who had now returned to their homes. The concrete blocks would, if laid in an edge-to-edge single line, extend for 83 miles. Over half a million cubic yards of clay, dug from 'borrow-pits' on Canvey had been deposited on the wall. Driven on a frontage of seawall of $5\frac{1}{2}$ miles were 2,000 tons of interlocking steel sheet piling. To reinforce the piling 5 miles of second-hand London tramrails had been used. Bedded in the seaward side were over a quarter of a million of the ubiquitous concrete blocks - a total of 350,000 of them.

The land echoed to the work of the men as they excavated, sank piling and laid clay. At the peak of the work there were 50 mechanical diggers, 20 bull

dozers and 70 lorries engaged. The labour strength
consisted of about 450 men.

Previously when flood ravages - on a smaller
scale - had had to be tackled there had been very
little in the way of mechanical labour. Horses and
carts were the most they could boast, plus the strong
muscles of British workmen. But now it was different.
Money and materials, men and machines, poured on to
the island to erect barricades the like of which had
never been known before. The work that had started in
those desperate months of 1953, reaching a climax in
May a year later, were to be continued until the
whole of the Island was girded by a massive ring of
steel, clay, concrete and bitumen.

The work so quickly accomplished was to be
inspected onn 15th May, 1954, by Her Majesty Queen
Elizabeth II, returning to the United Kingdom from a
successful Commonwealth Tour, in the Royal Yacht
Britannia escorted by the Daring class ships, *Duchess*
and *Decoy*. Midway between Shoeburyness and the Isle
of Sheppey they parted company with the Royal Yacht
and the escort was taken up by four Gay class fast-
patrol boats - *Gay Bombadier*, *Gay Charioteer*, *Gay
Charger* and *Gay Fencer*. As Her Majesty went up
river a 21 gun salute was fired from the Gun Saluting
Battery at Sheerness. Off Southend, the Trinity House
vessel *Patricia* took up station ahead of the *Britannia*
and a Port of London Authority barge, *Nore* advanced
ahead of *Patricia*. Three Metropolitan Police launches
joined the convoy later up-river.

Meanwhile, at Canvey, crowds thronged the
newly-finished seawalls. It became a huge natural
grandstand for this Royal event. Some people were so
determined not to miss it that they had camped out
all night on the wall. There were hundreds of boats
out on the water for the occasion. As the Royal
Yacht approached the Island's own flotilla of light
craft went out, led by Commodore Arthur Rapkin of
the Island Yacht Club.

On this splendid occasion one recalled a
grimmer time, 14 years before, when the Thames had
been alive with bobbing boats, yachts and light

cruisers. It was the evacuation of Dunkirk and then, as on that later celebration, Island men and boats were to the fore.

As the Yacht passed the Labworth Cafe a signal lamp, operated by Canvey Sea Scout leader Vic Ellis, flashed out a loyal message. Also on the flat roof of the cafe were gathered guests from mainland authorities, including the Essex County Council and the Essex River Board.

The Queen's return gave an opportunity for Eastern area, St John Ambulance Brigade, to put into operation new wireless-controlled mobile units, of which there were 19 along the Thames waterside from Southend to London, where crowds were expected to gather and where first aid posts were set up. These included 2 on Canvey, manned by personnel from Canvey & Benfleet and Southend Divisions, assisted by a contingent from other Essex Divisions.

The return also coincided with Canvey's local council elections, but business at most polling stations was very slack until later in the morning.

Canvey was now well on the way to recovery, but still world-wide generosity recognised the Island's hardship. Carpets, given by Canadians, were donated to residents who were living on the Island at the time of the flood. In June £20,000 was allocated by the Essex River Authority to improve certain hardcore roads laid after the flooding.

Canvey elected its first woman Council Chairman.

In that month the Council gave more details of seawall work that had been carried out and said, "The sea defences of the Island are now so improved that even in the remote chance of a tide reaching the top level of the new seawall, vast areas of London and parts of East Anglia would be under several feet of water, while the Island would remain dry."

Sea defence improvements had, by then, cost over three quarters of a million pounds. Loans for development on the Island sanctioned by Government Departments amounted to £375,000, while £76,000 had been advanced by Canvey Council for the purpose of building and buying property on the Island. Sir Thomas

Bohemia Hall

Dugdale, Minister of Agriculture, told Mr Braine in the House of Commons that Canvey's seawalls had been completed to above the standard recommended by the Waverley Committee.

Sporting prowess was still being shown by the Prout brothers who, with 8 others, represented Great Britain in the World Canoeing Championships in France in July. Francis and Roland had previously raced in France at an international regatta in Paris two years earlier.

In July there was further improvement news; a Whitehall loan for Thorney Bay improvements and authorisation had been received to go ahead with repairs to roads damaged in the floods and by evacuation vehicles. The scheme would cost £46,000* and repayment came through the flood fund. Already half a mile of the work had been completed.

It was also a memorable month for Henry Pettitt, aged 73, for on 3rd July he was retiring after 27 years as a travelling cinema proprietor. Mr Pettitt, who first started in the cinema business in 1905, ran Canvey's first cinema at the old 'Bohemia Hall', long since demolished. I well remember those days when we used to go to see Charlie Chaplin, Harold Lloyd, Tom Mix and other heroes and heroines of the silent screen. For, although 'talkies' had started, Mr Pettitt's films were of the sub-title variety - and no less good for that! Sometimes the films appeared through a 'rain-storm' of scratches, other times the films broke down, but we didn't mind. Times were lively, I recall on one occasion the lights going up and volunteers being called for to try to catch boys coming in without paying and to chuck them out. There were a few proper, tip-up seats at the back, but most other seating was bolted together chairs. Lemonade was available during the interval.

One never-to-be-forgotten event was the showing of *Captain Blood*. The first performance of this swashbuckling effort was marred - to an extent - because sub-titles were not available for some unknown reason. However, Mr Pettitt found it was such a

*Roads £32,000; Surface water drainage £8,000; Reinstatement works £4,000.

Girls' Bungalow Holiday Home, Lakeside Park. The lady with the rake is Miss Telford.

success that he decided to get sub-titles. All went well at their screening, except that in one dramatic sea-chase, one sea captain was seen to exclaim "Full steam ahead", as his opponent's sails disappeared over the horizon.

During the summer, when the films were shown, air conditioning was provided in the form of an old, wooden aeroplane propellor hanging from the ceiling.

Mr Pettitt had other gifts, he was a poet and an author. During the Great War he wrote a revue for the 34th Division and played in *Chu Chin Chow*.

The main work on Canvey's sea defences had been completed. Further improvement work was to be done at an estimated cost of £34,000.

Canvey's continuing appeal to holiday-makers was underlined with the development of Thorney Bay Beach Camp, which had made tremendous progress, now having 200 furnished chalets as well as caravan sites on 35 acres.

Canvey was settling down once again to its programme of sports, fetes, and, of course, its annual carnival, the 1954 procession being described as 'the best since the war'.

In August an Island pioneer died: she was Miss Clara Grace James, aged 87, who had come to Canvey in 1906 for a holiday. In 1909 she started a holiday home for working girls later to become a family holiday centre; during the winter it was a social club. A former Canvey Councillor and Justice of the Peace, Miss James found time to be a founder member, President and trustee (until 1951) of Canvey Women's Institute. She founded Canvey Labour Party and was connected with Canvey Nursing Association, being the President for some years. She also attended displays of Canvey Girls' Life Brigade at which she often presided. Miss James was the first woman to be elected to the London Trades Council. She gave evidence before a Royal Commission on Labour in the House of Commons, the outcome being the appointment of women factory inspectors.

Another 'pioneer' was to depart at the end of August, when a mystery fire gutted the 'Canvey' Club at Small Gains Corner. It had been the scene of many

The Methane Terminal

Benfleet & Canvey Island Regatta

LAND SPORTS, &c.,

WILL BE HELD

On SATURDAY, AUGUST 1st, 1908.

Holland-in-England.   Canvey Island, Essex.

Alight at Benfleet Station.   Fare from Southend, 3½d.

A unique Health Resort.   Beautiful Shell Beach, Good Bathing, Boating and Fishing.   A capital Harbour for yachts at Hole Haven. The far end of the Island confronts the German Ocean, commanding a fine view of the shipping continually passing.

Old Dutch Farms and Cottages.

An Ancient Well with thatched Roof stands in centre of the village.

Send for Scott's Illustrated Guide, Price 2d., post free.
SCOTT & CO., The Village, Canvey Island, Essex.

HOTEL KYNOCH, CANVEY ISLAND, SOUTH BENFLEET, ESSEX.

Board Residence from **6/=** per day. Week-End from **12/=** Table d'Hote Lunch **2/=** Bedrooms **2/6**
Finest Ales, Wines and Spirits. Best Brands of Tobacco, Cigars and Cigarettes. Billiards.
Large or Small Parties catered for on Special Terms.
Finest Position. Best Views. Produce from Own Farm.

TIME TABLE.
From SOUTHEND, WESTCLIFF and LEIGH to BENFLEET for CANVEY ISLAND.

Up.	a.m.	a.m	a.m	a.m.	a.m.	a.m.	a.m.	p.m.	p.m.	p.m.	p.m.	p.m.
Southend..	6 33	7 10	7 55	8 12	10 17	10 33	11 37	12 30*	12 55†	2 20	2 40	3 8†
Westcliff..	6 37	7 14	7 58	8 15	10 20	10 36	11 40	12 33	12 58	2 23	2 43	3 11
Leigh	6 41	7 19	8 3	8 20	10 24	10 41	11 41	12 38	1 3	2 28	2 48	3 15
Benfleet ..	6 49	7 27	8 11	8 28	10 32	10 49	11 52	12 47	1 11	2 36	2 56	3 23

Up.—contd.	p.m.	p.m.	p.m.	p.m.	p.m.	p.m.	p.m	p m.	p.m.	
Southend..	3 46*	4 33†	5 6	5 37†	6 12	7 18	7 58	9 5	9 15	* Not on Saturdays.
Westcliff..	3 49	4 36	5 9	5 40	6 15	7 21	8 1	9 8	9 18	
Leigh	3 54	4 41	5 14	5 45	6 19	7 25	8 6	9 12	9 22	† Saturdays only.
Benfleet ..	4 2	4 49	5 22	5 53	6 26	7 33	8 14	9 20	9 30	

SUNDAY.

Up.	a.m.	a.m.	p.m.	p.m.	p.m.	p.m.	p.m.	p.m.	p.m.
Southend..	8 38	10 7	2 14	4 28	5 53	6 57	7 5	7 58	8 47
Westcliff..	8 41	10 10	2 17	4 31	5 56	7 0	7 8	8 1	8 50
Leigh	8 45	10 14	2 21	4 35	6 0	7 4	7 12	8 5	8 55
Benfleet ..	8 53	10 22	2 29	4 43	6 8	7 12	7 20	8 13	9 3

From BENFLEET to LEIGH, WESTCLIFF and SOUTHEND.

Down.—Benfleet .. a.m.: 6.41, 7.28, 9.22, 9.33, 10.58, 11.35; p.m.: 12.4, 1.21, 1.34, 2.13 (Sats. only), 3.11 (Sats. only), 3.44, 4.7 (Sats. only), 4.48, 5.9, 5.28, 6 40, 7.22 (not Sats.), 7.37 (not Sats.), 8.15 (Sats. only), 8.30 (not Sats.), 9.47.

SUNDAY.
Down.—Benfleet .. a.m.: 10 25, 11.5, 11.41, 11.29 (Midland); p.m.: 12.46, 3.43, 4.4, 7.26, 9.25, 10.14

Benfleet & Canvey Island Regatta & Land Sports, Saturday, Aug. 1st, 1908

social occasions and other gatherings, such as ratepayers' meetings.

And so the years of progress continue. Canvey's
increasing attractions as a residential and seaside
resort became even more apparent. First the building
of new houses and estates and then, as land became
scare, infilling - the buying and demolition of the
older types of property (constructed, I was once
assured, in a 'non-traditional way'. An evocative
phrase that has lingered in my memory like that of
'ponding of the terrain' - officialese for road
puddles). Industrialisation and controversial plans to
build oil refineries, the resistance to these latter
schemes making headlines in local and national
newspapers.

For the visitors Newlands Holiday Camp became
a centre of attraction and the long-delayed plan to
build a Canvey Town Centre has been accomplished.

Throughout the years, the keynote has been
progress, sometimes against extreme odds. The Island
has been written off, only to make a come-back. Its
administration and local government has altered over
the years, even its shape has not remained constant
with the sea invading, being driven back, more land
being reclaimed. Its barriers have been strengthened
over the years and the struggle continues to keep
intact what has been wrested from the sea.

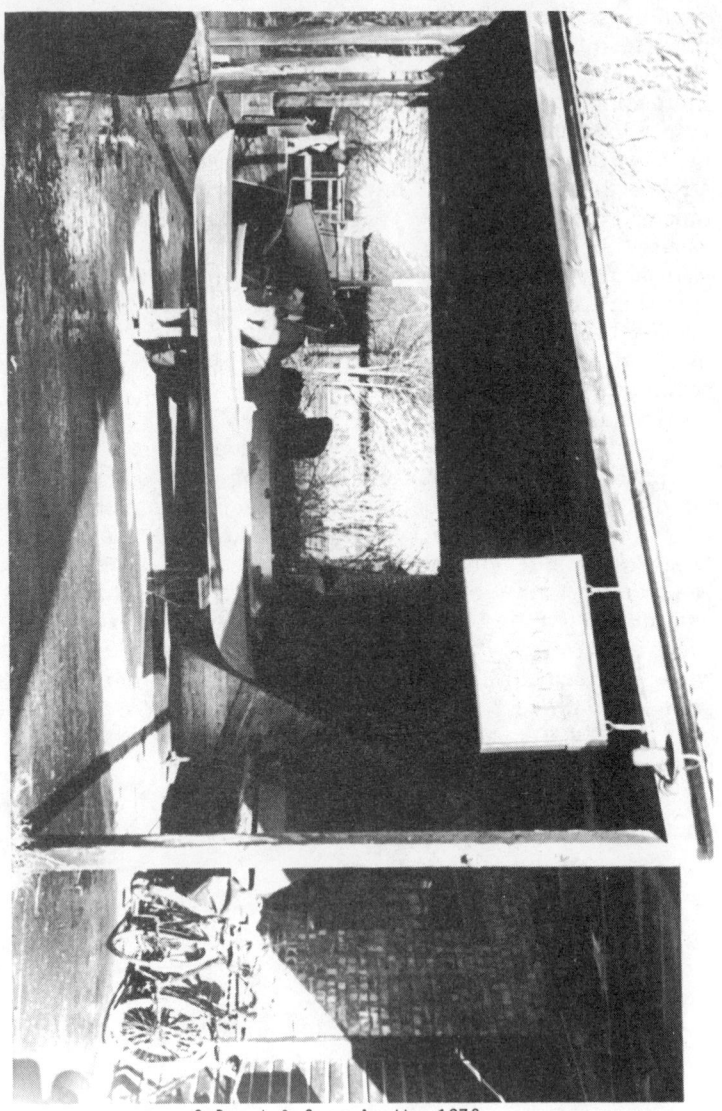

G Prout & Sons in the 1930s

AFTERWORD

Looking back over the years - and reading the proofs of this manuscript - it is hard to believe that Canvey Island is the same place. However, on thinking back, some of the Island's characteristics remain.

The heavy industrialisation of Canvey has always been strongly resisted by its residents. It started in the early 30s with the construction of oil storage tanks at Hole Haven (the first place to be bombed in 1940) and recommenced in the 60s with plans for oil refineries and the continued storage of methane (natural) gas.

After a series of public enquiries into the proposed refineries planning permission was granted to the American firm of Occidental, Ltd., and the Italian company United Refineries, Ltd. Visible sign of the American development got under way, but ceased, leaving it half finished at a cost of £M64. United Refineries' land has not been built on, although there is a roadway leading to it from Canvey Road. These installations are in the western part of the island, where the chief attraction is the deep water of the Thames, the up-river haul towards London being shortened considerably. The methane storage has also been much scaled down. The Texaco oil storage installation was announced as closing in 1985.

Light industry has been happier. Again in the western part of the island, there is a large factory estate, ranging from the very large down to one or two man nursery units, the latter encouraged by successive Councils. At the other end of the island is a further industrial estate, where is housed the world famous catamaran boat builders, Prouts. This was the firm that gave much-needed help in 1953, when many of their smaller craft were used for rescue work.

To provide skilled workers, technicians, craft people and clerical staff, the long-established Tower Radio, Ltd., started Canvey Island and District Training Centre, working with the government's Youth Training Scheme: currently there are 300 on its books, with 24 instructors. One of its projects has been the restoration

Furtherwick

of The Lake as a wild-life habitat and beauty spot.

Both industrial estates have been developed from open farm land and the inherent problems of drainage have been overcome to provide thriving communities.

House building has gone on and, to overcome the shortage of land, many older properties have been demolished, new houses appearing in their place. To the north there is still an area, known as Sixty Acres, which is one of the first parts developed by Frederick Hester and this now is growing. Of course, should the oil companies not resume their schemes, their large land holdings would come on to the market.

A hospital is still not available in the area, despite increasing pressure from local organisations and residents. Money collected for a hospital project was used to open a centre for the handicapped after the larger scheme was turned down. Schools have kept pace with growing demand under the auspices of Essex County Council.

There has been no lack of commercial development in other spheres. The days of the first Barclays Bank, a wooden hut crouching under the sheltering arms of the elm trees at Small Gains Corner, are long since past. In the flood of 1953 the bank was driven out of its premises, then at Lakeside Corner: now it has a new centre with a pleasing exterior based on a Dutch style.

Building societies have opened branches on the Island and estate agents' offices proliferate. Shops have developed with the building of a large shopping hall in Furtherwick Road - with a population approaching 40,000, they are needed!

Amenities have reached a stage undreamt of 30 years ago. The Council has expanded Waterside Farm sports complex at a cost of £M1 and the Paddocks Community Centre in the heart of the Island is in continual use. It is interesting to note that this sports complex embraces a former farm and the community centre is sited on a piece of land formerly used for pony riding.

Local organisations have flourished. Canvey Carnival celebrated its diamond jubilee in 1985; Canvey Lifeguards have a rebuilt headquarters; the Horticultural Society members continue to stage shows, having long ago overcome the deluge of seawater into their gardens in 1953 that killed so many earthworms that they had to be 'imported' from the mainland. Castle Point and District Endeavour Clubs, based on the Island, still give a welcome service for the physically and mentally handi capped, as well as for the lonely; the Rotary and Lions' Clubs do good work for local charities; senior citizens are cared for by branches of the National Federation of Old Age Pensioners' Associations and a day centre. This has named but a few of the varied organisations that cater for an ever-increasing range of interests and causes.

On the amusement side, visitors continue to flock to the Island to enjoy the facilities of two well-run holiday camps.

Since the dawn of the Island's history sea defences have played a vital role. The seawall was rebuilt after the 1953 disaster, as earlier recounted. Because of the construction of the Woolwich Flood Barrier, walls down-river would, if there was a tidal surge necessitating the Barrier being closed, come under pressure. The Anglian Water Authority therefore rebuilt them again, raising their height. The new massive concrete and steel bulwark combines an outer sea wall promenade and a walk-way on the inner side, as well as a broad path along the top. Additionally, two of the creeks have barriers; one of them, at the western side of the Island, is to be used to provide extra emergency ways on and off the Island. The new defences have been built at a cost of £M34.

Reminders of the Island's past remain. The historic inn, the Lobster Smack; the two Dutch cottages, one a museum, the other in private ownership; the former St Katherine's parish church is now a heritage centre and museum; the former coastguard station, with its cottages, is still at the sea end of Haven Road, although there are fears for the future of the listed buildings.

Churches are flourishing and a new plan is under way at the present parish church of St Nicholas for a family centre to include the parish church and hall.

Perhaps it would be well to conclude with the Reverend Tim Stevens' words on this project: "So the history of our Island has been one of constant change and adapting to new needs" [with my proviso - that we also need to keep our old virtues and values].

Ferry from Benfleet to Canvey.

The Ferry, c.1905